Troubled Everyday

The Aesthetics of Violence and the Everyday in European Art Cinema

Alison Taylor

EDINBURGH
University Press

For mum 1957–2013

Edinburgh University Press is one of the leading university presses in the UK. We publish academic books and journals in our selected subject areas across the humanities and social sciences, combining cutting-edge scholarship with high editorial and production values to produce academic works of lasting importance. For more information visit our website: edinburghuniversitypress.com

© Alison Taylor, 2017

Edinburgh University Press Ltd
The Tun – Holyrood Road
12 (2f) Jackson's Entry
Edinburgh EH8 8PJ
www.euppublishing.com

Typeset in 11/13 Monotype Ehrhardt by
Servis Filmsetting Ltd, Stockport, Cheshire

A CIP record for this book is available from the British Library

ISBN 978 1 4744 1522 4 (hardback)
ISBN 978 1 4744 1523 1 (webready PDF)
ISBN 978 1 4744 1524 8 (epub)

The right of Alison Taylor to be identified as author of this work has been asserted in accordance with the Copyright, Designs and Patents Act 1988 and the Copyright and Related Rights Regulations 2003 (SI No. 2498).

Contents

Acknowledgements iv
List of Figures v

1 'A lightning that illuminates the banal': Violence and the Everyday 1
2 Everyday Moments 16
3 Everyday Style 37
4 Everyday Structures/Everyday Language 60
5 Return to the Everyday 89
Conclusion: Looking Back 117

Works Cited 125
Filmography 132
Index 135

Acknowledgements

This book began as the flicker of an idea with the encouragement of my friend and mentor Jason Jacobs. Thank you for many years of conversation. I could not have completed this book without your guidance.

Thanks also to my friends, family and colleagues – your understanding, kind-heartedness, reassurance and support both kept me sane and encouraged me to persist in following my interests.

I wish to express my gratitude to Gillian Leslie and the team at Edinburgh University Press for their guidance and support.

A very special thank you to my dear friend John Edmond, whose love of cinema never fails to spur on my own. Your generosity and advice is most appreciated.

My gratitude also goes out to Catherine Wheatley, Tanya Horeck, Greg Hainge, Lisa Bode, Joseph Clowes and Elliott Logan, who have all been a part of this trek with me in their own way.

And finally to Bec McKenzie whose belief in me was unwavering, who saw things she cannot unsee, and whose own everyday was often disrupted as a result.

Figures

2.1	Orazio Gentileschi, *Lot and His Daughters*, c. 1622 (digital image courtesy of the Getty's Open Content Program)	22
2.2	Watching characters watching in *Salò*	25
2.3	Gesturing beyond the frame – the pianist's unrequited gaze in *Salò*	28
2.4	Retreat into the ordinary – the final image of *Salò*	30
2.5–2.6	Lot's Wife – Glasha looks back in *Come and See*	34
3.1–3.2	Fragments of everyday banality in *The Seventh Continent*	48
3.3–3.4	Analogous framing – fragments of self-destruction	49
3.5–3.6	Broken lamps and bloodied walls – violence is displaced onto everyday objects in *Money*	52
3.7	Textual openness writ large in the final shot of *Money*	56
4.1	Beautiful and overwhelming – the desert as sublime in *Twentynine Palms*	74
4.2	The earth abides – the final shot in *Twentynine Palms*	76
4.3	Sisterly bonding in *Fat Girl*	81
4.4	The earth stops – the freeze-frame that ends *Fat Girl*	86
5.1–5.4	Narrativised time – excerpts from the opening montage in *I Stand Alone*	96–7
5.5	Aestheticisation of the everyday – the closing of *I Stand Alone*	103
5.6	A history of abuse filtered through the banal – the casual reveal of Wolfgang's many letters in *Michael*	111
5.7	The routine replaces the dramatic in *Michael*	113
6.1	The everyday upturned in *Irreversible*	122

CHAPTER I

'A lightning that illuminates the banal': Violence and the Everyday

> Things flash up – little worlds, bad impulses, events alive with some kind of charge. Sudden eruptions are fascinating beyond all reason, as if they're divining rods articulating something. But what? (Kathleen Stewart, *Ordinary Affects*, 68)

A mother and her two teenage daughters are resting at a roadside stop when a madman smashes through the windshield of their sedan to crush the eldest girl's skull with a hatchet. An insurance broker interrupts his otherwise banal evening to rape the small boy he holds captive in his basement, then marks the event in a day planner. A widowed housewife systematically carries out her domestic duties, including prostituting herself, before stabbing a client to death with a pair of scissors. A petit-bourgeois family sit down to a lavish meal only to then destroy all their belongings and commit suicide.

In each of these extreme moments[1] it is the domestic, the familial and the routine that serves as their setting and currency. Brushing teeth, getting ready for and going to work, watching television, smoking cigarettes, shopping for groceries, doing the laundry – all those little cumulative non-events that populate day-to-day life, that in most films are effaced or at least dulled to a kind of background noise to furnish 'real drama', are here made prominent. It is not that these films are devoid of action, rather, when the dramatic does occur it ruptures the viewing experience with such unparalleled acerbity that it gives one cause to reflect on what was actually at stake in the commonplace.

This book is about the tension between violence and the everyday in European art cinema.[2] It is about perceived excesses, seemingly meaningless acts of violence which when scrutinised are found to be inextricably connected to the everyday. And it is about the ways in which these films invite us to, and then thwart us from reconciling these two poles, preventing us closing down the emotions they elicit into a contained whole.

The films observed in the pages to follow employ violent disruptions to the everyday that throw into focus a troubling inability to understand the world and others. Far from being shock for shock's sake, I argue that these violent punctures speak to a fundamental human desire for meaning. The patterning of the everyday in these films, as something vulnerable to violent disruptions capable of revealing epistemological uncertainty, is intrinsic to their capacity to disturb; these films are troubling because they question our relation to the world, and the patterns and routines by which we make sense of it.

Take, for example, a scene that occurs towards the end of Michael Haneke's *Hidden* (2005). The Laurent family – husband Georges, wife Anne, and teenage son Pierrot have been receiving anonymous video cassette recordings: surveillance of their home and private conversations. Georges suspects a figure from his childhood whom he has wronged. However, when confronted, Majid denies all knowledge of the mysterious tapes. Later, Majid calls Georges to meet with him at his tenement, presumably to reveal some new information. However, after inviting him inside, in a startling moment, Majid unexpectedly slits his own throat. Blood bursts at once in a fine mist and a thick torrent, staining the drab wall in a vivid red stripe as his body collapses to the floor, his head unceremoniously hitting a chair on his way down. Georges stares stunned at the blood spreading across the floor at a barely perceptible measure towards him. Majid labouredly gurgles on the floor like a congested snorer, Georges gasps, paces, coughs. There is nothing in Majid's performance prior to this act, nor in the film's style, to indicate that this will happen. The moment occurs in a static long take, its shock accumulating weight through the time it is held onscreen. This sudden irruption of violence into the everyday seems to signal something profound; it occurs at the moment when we expect the film's central enigma might be resolved and its narrative to most cohere. What we witness, however, is a gruesome spectacle, an arresting caesura of style. Instead of the clarity we anticipate, this suicide continues and deepens the existing openness of meaning that characterises the film as a whole.

In its representation of violence, this scene exemplifies some of the qualities that I take to be at the core of the films examined in the pages to follow: it is unexpected and de-dramatised (we are not afforded the aural cues to imminent brutality familiar in a horror film, nor does the *mise-en-scène* give us any indication that violence is likely); it is staged in an everyday setting (such as a home, school or workplace); the violence is perpetrated by a person (as opposed to a monster or supernatural force); and while its gravity seems to suggest a deeper significance, it is neither clearly motivated nor easily reconcilable to the narrative we have been presented with thus far.

Kartik Nair (2009) describes Majid's suicide as 'an act of violence so unbelievable we hit rewind'. Drawing on Walter Benjamin's metaphor of the constellation to describe the impact of this moment, Nair argues its abruptness is like a flash of lightning; past and present are united in this moment of excess so at odds with the rest of the film. Similarly, Lisa Coulthard describes Majid's suicide, and a similar instance of sudden violence in Haneke's *The Piano Teacher* (2001), as effecting a 'surplus that reveals the fundamental shortcomings of knowledge or comprehension' (2009: 47). Evident in both scholars' reactions is a sense that the abrupt violence is excessive, without clear meaning, and involves us in some way – in Nair's assessment, our response is to rewind, in Coulthard's we are compelled to respond, and yet our ability to do so is simultaneously blocked; 'There is no "proper" response immediately at hand' (Coulthard 2009: 47).

That a man unexpectedly slitting his throat onscreen might make for disturbing viewing goes without saying. Everyday patterns, the habits and routines that constitute social order, are designed precisely to minimise the potential for disruption and uncertainty. It is in the arrangement of daily life that we might stave off the threat of disorder, and 'preserve a sense of the continuity and reliability of things' (Silverstone 1994: 1). And yet, if the external pressures of an unknown observer, or invitation to a gruesome suicide, might strike us as being very much antithetical to the routines and repetitions of everyday life, it is of no small significance that Haneke's film finds its affective currency within this realm. By focusing on the family unit, its marital and parental tensions, and of reconciling one's past actions with the present, *Hidden*'s unprecedented burst of violence unsettles the foundations of the very institutions that we rely upon to craft and maintain our identities.

Over the coming chapters, I consider the implications of the fusillade of violence into the everyday as a kind of meaning-blocking event – a dynamic that I take to be central to a significant strand of contemporary European art cinema. Such a dynamic is neither hospitable to a tidy definition, nor simply reducible to art film ambiguity, as it is deployed in varied and complex ways. Instead, *Troubled Everyday* demonstrates that it is indeed an observable aesthetic mechanism, and a rich source of insight into the nature of why these films are so emotionally significant. I argue that these films gesture towards the profound; that the intrusion of violence into everyday spaces, and our own uncomfortable involvement, suggests the potential to reveal something about human nature, and yet the significance or meaning of this violence remains deliberately undefined. The achievement of these films is that their handling of the tension between violence and the everyday refuses attempts at hermeneutic closure, and instead extends the films' disturbance beyond the moment of consumption into our own everyday lives.

FROM EXTREMISM TO EVERYDAY

The tendency towards provocative and confronting European art cinema[3] has, since the late 1990s, garnered a renewed attention. Now well documented, this tendency has recently attracted a variety of labels, including the 'new European cinema' (Falcon 1999), 'new French extremity' (Quandt 2004), '*cinéma du corps*' (Palmer 2006, 2011), 'cinema of sensation' (Beugnet 2007), 'new extremism' (Horeck and Kendall 2011), 'unwatchable' (Grønstad 2007, 2012) and 'feel-bad film' (Lübecker 2011b, 2015). Far from being a cohesive cinematic entity or unified movement, the films associated with these terms are perhaps best linked by a wilful sense of transgression that plays out in varying ways. This might pertain to the transgression of genre expectations, as in the shocking subversion of the family-under-threat narrative in Haneke's *Funny Games* (1997/ 2007), or Bruno Dumont's affront to the American road movie in *Twentynine Palms* (2003). In other cases, it may be the transgression of a tidy division between art and exploitation, high and low taste. By extension, it is the blurring of boundaries between auteur and popular. And finally, transgression has also been argued to occur in the muddling of a clear division between spectator and screen – a kind of sensory immersion (see Beugnet 2007; Palmer 2011) or uncomfortable ethical involvement (see Lübecker 2015; Wheatley 2009).

While indebted to this scholarship, and engaging with several films that have been attributed to this trend, I should state up front that this is not a book *about* the 'new extremism' per se. It is, rather, an account of a strand in the broader history of violence in European art cinema; one that intersects with and, I hope, contributes to our understanding of contemporary as well as historical extremes. In part, it is an attempt to reconcile my own experience of these films with what I perceive to be an under-explored avenue in the existing literature on violence in European art cinema. While a great deal of attention has rightly been paid to moments of extremity, particularly to filmmakers' aggressive gestures to rupture the viewing experience, little has been said of the contextual frameworks that these moments puncture. Where scholars have broached the everyday, the focus has been relatively limited; either to a particular filmmaker, as in Coulthard's (2011) insightful reflection on the blending of extremity and banality in the films of Michael Haneke;[4] or to single chapters in larger studies, for example Grønstad's consideration of transgressive moments in films which otherwise ascribe to the tendencies of slow cinema,[5] or Lübecker's (2015) account of an affective 'unease', amid a larger study of possible 'feel-bad' experiences.[6]

What is the significance of the everyday that surrounds moments of sudden unexpected violence? Why do these films seem to rely so heavily upon everyday settings and patterns for their impact? In seeking to answer these questions, this book extends the discussion of cinema violence as something that engages with or emerges out of the seemingly insignificant patterns of the day-to-day. *Troubled Everyday* recasts attention to the role of the everyday within extreme cinema, calling for an approach that is attentive to the ordinary as well as the exceptional.

Of course, the everyday is a varied thing, open to multiple and at times conflicting definitions. It is a matter of content; the routines and repetitions that in these films fill so much screen time. At other times, it is also an aesthetic sensibility, patently undramatic. As a concept in cultural studies, philosophy and aesthetics it has been conceived of both in positive and negative terms. However, I will argue that what allies these particular films so strongly to the everyday is their affinity with indeterminacy, what Michael Sheringham calls the everyday's 'fruitful ambivalence' (2006: 30).

In negative conceptions, everydayness is associated with the inconsequential, the fruitless and the spurious, in contrast to what is significant and eventful. Regarded this way, the everyday renders us passive – it is something we necessarily endure, and something 'we must extricate ourselves from if we are to live authentically' (Sheringham 2006: 23). This extrication might come in the form of aesthetic experience via high art, or modernist movements like Surrealism that jolt the senses and render the familiar strange. Such encounters with art are thought to disrupt the everyday's circadian temporality, awakening perception from mindless habit (Felski 2002: 608).

For Georg Lukács, release comes in the form of extraordinary and miraculous moments that wrench us from the 'numbness' of the ordinary:

> Real life is always unreal, always impossible, in the midst of empirical life. Suddenly there is a gleam, a lightning that illuminates the banal paths of empirical life: something disturbing and seductive, dangerous and surprising; the accident, the great moment, the miracle; an enrichment and a confusion. It cannot last, no one would be able to bear it, no one could live at such heights – at the height of their own life and their own ultimate possibilities. One has to fall back into numbness. (1974: 153)

Here Lukács distinguishes between the banality of the everyday and the elevated sphere of 'real life'. Paroxysmal instants interrupt the monotonous to reveal the genuine, and in such transcendent moments we might 'attempt to glimpse the totality of things' (Aitken 2006: 70).

One can see how a connection might be drawn to the structural division that the films under scrutiny employ – between day-to-day patterns and developments, and their sudden disturbance. The gruesome spectacle of Majid's suicide, or the catalogue of quotidian violence that opens this introduction, not only disrupt any sense of complacency, but seem to confront us with something comparatively significant.[7] The violence in these films strikes like Lukács' lightning, only the path that is illuminated is anything but clear.

In negative conceptions of the everyday, profundity is located outside of everyday life, antithetical to its alienating structures and impositions. More positive views of the everyday, however, take issue with this equation. Henri Lefebvre, for instance, contends that the everyday is not simply a vacuum in wait of the marvellous. Instead, he argues that by attending to the microstructures of everyday life, positive aspects of the quotidian can be rescued from those that alienate (Lefebvre 2008 VI: 42). Likewise, Michel de Certeau has argued that despite its constraints, the everyday is filled with creative potential. For de Certeau oppressive structures and mechanisms are subverted daily by ordinary people who adapt them for their own purposes. For example, he compares the pedestrian's reappropriation of city streets – with their implicit limitations on one's movement – into shortcuts and detours to the manifold possibilities improvised in Charlie Chaplin's cane which is transformed, going 'beyond the limits that the determinants of the object set on its utilization' (1984: 98).

Reclaiming the quotidian from its alienating aspects is integral to Stanley Cavell's conception of the everyday, which is rooted in a need to reconnect with the world by acknowledging the ordinary. Such a reading is at the heart of Cavell's 'threat of skepticism', based on the idea that modern human consciousness has become dislocated from the world in the absence of certainty, disrupted in the principles of reasoning and empiricism forwarded in the Renaissance and Enlightenment (1999: 440). The effect is something of a paradoxical yearning; the need to attain the world facilitates our flight from it. One might contrast Cavell's notion here to Lukács' evocation of 'the accident, the great moment, the miracle' that momentarily relieves us from the numbness of the ordinary. While Lukács speaks longingly of this disruptive instant that would take us out of the everyday, central to Cavell's thinking is a call for us to overcome this longing, and to discover the fascination in everyday life, for it is here that we might know ourselves and others. Accordingly, for Cavell and others who conceive the everyday in positive terms, profundity is found in 'the near, the low, the common', rather than our avoidance of it (Emerson 1982: 101).

Amid positive and negative conceptions of the everyday, and adding to the difficulty of defining it, is the view that the everyday rests in an inherent sense of indeterminacy, simultaneously perplexing and self-evident. Maurice Blanchot argues that the everyday is fraught with paradoxical ambiguity; nothing happens, and yet something is always happening (1993: 241); it escapes apprehension (ibid.: 239), and yet it is 'what we are first of all and most often' (ibid.: 238). For Sheringham, this kind of indeterminacy is crucial to the everyday, as taking a strictly positive or strictly negative stance 'is to filter out the tensions that give the everyday its fruitful ambivalence, and above all its status as a sphere of human self-realization' (2006: 30). As Rita Felski warns, everyday life should not be considered as a comprehensive object, as no life is definitively anchored in the everyday, and that to assume so would 'impose a fantasy of sameness' (2002: 29).

Looking at these films through the lens of varied conceptions of the everyday is similarly fraught with ambiguity. On the one hand, we might consider everyday structures as a shield from contingency. The familial and domestic, the institutions and patterns we establish, can be seen as the contained, familiar and stable, erected to shelter us from the unknown and volatile outside. It is this very tension between established patterns of being and the potential for turmoil that can be found in the films explored in this book. Instances of violence in these films are rendered disturbing for their seeming break with the continuity of everyday patterns and the sense-making constructs we impose on daily life. Alternatively, one could argue that where ordering the everyday might seek to suppress violence, it in fact acts as a breeding ground. The clinical treatment of routine tasks in *The Seventh Continent* (Haneke 1989) or the lifeless performance of household duties in *Jeanne Dielman* (Akerman 1975) seem to propose such a reading, both films culminating in violence. However, I argue that these films complicate binaries of the everyday as positive or negative, shields or incubators for violence, and instead explore the way the indeterminacy of their narratives compliments evocations of the everyday as itself indefinite. Moments of violence are flashes of lightning illuminating the everyday; they gesture towards a profound significance and yet, as I will demonstrate, the stylistic and structural methods employed are marked by a refusal to define the meaning of this violence and offer closure.

In evoking the everyday in cinema, there are of course also links to the similarly complicated concept of 'realism'. Much of the purchase these films have is garnered through their relationship to our sense of daily life, through the emphasis on familiar activities and routines. The relationship between 'realism' and 'the everyday' remains a recurring concern throughout the book. For now, though, I want to consider realism not in the sense of the mimetic relationship between artistic representations and the world, but rather in the metaphysical sense. To consider realism in art is to enter 'into questions of ontology and epistemology: of what exists in the world, and how that world can be known' (Lovell 1983: 6). It is, as Christopher Williams articulates, to make the distinction between the truth of what we perceive, and an 'essential truth' which is not so much observed as it is 'born of the mind' (1980: 11). Questions of profundity and the location of authentic experience are an enduring concern for theoreticians of the everyday. As noted earlier, for thinkers like Emerson and Cavell, such questions are framed in terms of acknowledgement

– that in cleaving to the everyday, 'the near, the low', we might reconnect with and know the world; for Lukács, as well as other thinkers like Georges Bataille (1986), they are framed in terms of escape – that in a rupturing moment we might transcend the ordinary and access a kind of hidden totality.[8]

My point is that at work in the screen aesthetics of these films is a dynamic whereby this tension between violence and meaning is played out for us, and left unresolved. We neither overcome the yearning for certainty, to make peace with the everyday and the limits of our knowledge as Cavell and Emerson would have us do, nor do we achieve that sublime sense of transcendence or transfiguration that Lukács longs for. Instead, we experience these two poles in tension; in various ways these films entice us to draw meaning from sudden acts of violence, and then work to preclude us from doing so. In these films, violence is the element that makes this feeling of uncertainty perceptible – either with sudden precision as in the case of Majid's suicide, or as a gradual encroachment as in the films explored in Chapter 2. Whether subtle or explicit, this dynamic functions to open a disturbing gap between violence and meaning.

APPROACHING DISTURBING AESTHETICS

Articulating what I mean by the 'disturbing' involves a tricky balance between affect and aesthetics. To make claims about the way certain films seek to involve us is necessarily to engage with questions of affect. As Carl Plantinga notes, affect remains a rather broad term,[9] generally denoting 'felt bodily states' that might include anything ranging from sensations, emotions and moods to reactions (Plantinga 2009a: 87). Intuitively, studies of extreme cinema have drawn upon theories of affect as a means to account for the often challenging responses such cinema generates.[10] However, affect need not be limited to describing intense emotions; as I will develop in Chapter 2, the concept of affect and its relationship to form can also help to describe more mild or lasting responses.

While at times utilising shock tactics, the films explored in this book are predominantly concerned with evoking a lingering sense of unease. And yet, I am still inclined to frame the current project primarily in terms of aesthetics for two reasons. First, while there is a long history of theorisation regarding how films might involve us via character alignment, identification and distanciation,[11] as I will demonstrate, the aesthetic I describe is not limited to character, structure or mode of address; rather, it spans all of these in complex ways. Second, I am wary of a tendency in some (by no means all) affect-based theory to immerse oneself so completely in one's subjective experience as to render the film under observation as secondary. Eugenie Brinkema (2014: 30) cautions against this tendency, arguing that the turn to affect need not be a turn away from form, warning that affect-based readings should resist a desire to reactively overcompensate for the monolithic assumptions about audiences made under screen theory in the 1970s by over-privileging the individual and exceptional.

Following Brinkema's lead, the approach taken in this book seeks to redress the balance between a too-distant and unstirred formalism, and overly agitated and unreflective modes of affect theory. It is, akin to Brinkema's intervention, a matter of '*reading for form*' (in a move back towards 'the specificity, complexity, and sensitivity to textuality that has gone missing in affect studies'), and '*reading affects as having forms*' (that is, to de-privilege 'models of expressivity and interiority in favor of treating affects as structures that work through formal means') (Brinkema 2014: 37). This is to treat affectivity as something that is expressed through film form, and, by virtue of its capacity to be externalised, to regard it as 'something that commands a reading' (Brinkema 2014: 4).

The real core of my argument pertains to an aesthetic mechanism, the way in which violence and the everyday are held in tension so as to preclude tethering the former to a reconcilable and reassuring meaning. As Frederick Luis Aldama asserts, 'artists, directors, architects, novelists, and so on use devices to give shape to discomforting art; they look for shapes that will unsettle us and take us away from our comfort zone' (Aldama and Lindenberger 2016: 8). *Troubled Everyday* is an attempt to account for one of these shapes, examining what I take to be a recurrent patterning of screen aesthetics in European art cinema.

The link between textual ambiguity and unpleasant emotional involvement in relation to examples of contemporary European cinema is not in itself novel. Much of the scholarship dedicated to films associated with the new extremism articulates a dynamic whereby the spectatorial position is complicated, often in uncomfortable ways, by a degree of textual openness. For Martine Beugnet (2007), this openness occurs in the textural quality of films that privilege corporeal sensation over traditional character and narrative, evident in their ability to trigger our senses beyond the visual and aural. Grønstad likewise describes 'unwatchable' films as lacking a sense of aesthetic containment, 'as if their violent energy has burst through the membrane of the work to target the spectators themselves' (2012: 2). More recently still, Lübecker considers the ethical and pedagogical potential of the 'feel-bad' film experience: one that generates a desire for catharsis, only to deny its satisfaction (2015: 2). What *Troubled Everyday* shares with this scholarship is a desire to account for the ways that particular strands of contemporary art cinema typify a viewing experience that is uncomfortably proximate. Ultimately, this book aims to contribute to the ongoing dialogue about the nature of cinema violence, extending these avenues of thought about the affective potential of extreme moments into a detailed conversation with the everyday that they puncture.

The approach I take in the following chapters is guided by the two aims of this book: to demonstrate a tendency in recent European art cinema to hold the everyday in tension with violence, and to articulate the various ways such an aesthetic patterning plays out. My approach therefore is one dedicated first and foremost to an analysis of film style. It is an attempt to reconnect with a given film 'on its own terms' (Clayton 2011: 36). That is, to use language to engage with films in their complexity, rather than to treat them as puzzles to be solved; it is to acknowledge, not to master. I demonstrate the films' disturbing qualities through evocatively describing the films themselves. This is not to argue that 'the viewer' is a cohesive category that can be said to respond in delimited ways determined by the text, rather it is to posit that the films examined in this book are designed to encourage discomfort in the audience through observable aesthetic choices; it is to read affect as having form.[12]

At the same time, while I maintain that disturbing aesthetics represent observable qualities in a number of films, I do not mean to suggest that such a mechanism is a predictable feature. As a point of comparison, it is worth considering Andrew Goldstone's description of the 'knight's move' as a literary device employed by Vladimir Nabokov. Serving as a metaphor for an evasive style, the knight in chess does not move in a straight line, but changes course and can skip over those in its way, unlike any other piece. Goldstone refers to a recurring device in Nabokov's style strategically employed 'to frustrate your expectations, to leap over the apparently important events into something else characterized by a kind of aesthetic play'. This sense of play is crucial because while often employed, the 'knight's move' is not a predictable mechanism but functions in a variety of ways. Similarly, where the mechanism I describe creates a gap between violent representation and its significance, it is evinced across various aspects of the text (structure, mode of address, temporality and so on), and, as is elucidated in detail in Chapter 4, is not a formulaic device but subject to nuance.

Because of my focus on the disturbing as an aesthetic mechanism, the chapters that follow engage in detailed case studies. However, this is not to say that this patterning is limited only to the films explored here. Rather, these case studies are indicative of a larger trend, and through these case studies we can both observe the greater pattern and the nuances of each individual film. Where relevant, I will refer to other comparable examples that similarly pursue the patterns and tensions raised to demonstrate this theory's wider relevance. At its broadest level, for instance, we could expand this corpus to consider the significance of everyday aspects in several other examples of films primarily thought of in terms of extremity. The family unit and its capacity for violence is observable in several films that are not explored in detail here, such as *Fists in the Pocket* (Bellocchio 1965), *My Mother* (Honoré 2004), *Dogtooth* (Lanthimos

2009) and *Bastards* (Denis 2013), among others. By extension, one could also examine the relationship between violence and the day-to-day in small communities in films that similarly temper style in ways comparable to the films examined in Chapter 3, as in *Humanity* (Dumont 1999), *The White Ribbon* (Haneke 2009) and *The Tribe* (Slaboshpytskyi 2014). Alternatively, there are evocations of this tension that spill over into the fantastic that fall outside of my scope here, but that may warrant further consideration, as in Lars von Trier's supernaturally tinged tale of a married couple in grief – *Antichrist* (2009), and Andrzej Zulawski's Surrealist rendering of domestic dysfunction as otherworldly in *Possession* (1981).

I begin in Chapter 2 by seeking to reframe the way in which we might consider the affective potential of extreme cinema by investigating an implicit dynamic at work in its reception: the distinction between an immediate visceral response and a more pervasive and enduring kind of affect. The chapter then turns to extreme works that I take to be significant precursors to the aesthetic dynamic that pitches violence and the everyday in tension, albeit in more discreet ways. While it may seem counterintuitive to begin a study of everyday style with films that are set in undeniably extreme circumstances, both Pier Paolo Pasolini's *Salò or the 120 Days of Sodom* (1975) and Elem Klimov's *Come and See* (1985) provide an interesting inversion of the aesthetic that informs the remaining chapters. I argue that in foregrounding extreme violence, the films' subtle gestures towards the everyday at key moments prove crucial to their affective quality, and signal that the distinction between the extreme and the everyday is not necessarily clear-cut.

Where Chapter 2 deals with ordinary moments in extraordinary films, Chapter 3 explores another aspect of the spectrum of the everyday in cinema: the concept of the everyday as a film style, and its relationship to the everyday as subject matter. This chapter examines the way the everyday as film style has been theorised – predominantly as an aesthetic sensibility that privileges the undramatic and routine as a conduit to the profound or transcendent. Chapter 3 asserts that while this scholarship has been useful in illuminating positive representations of the everyday, its attempts to quarantine the everyday from the dramatic are problematic and ultimately reductive; stringent definitions that hold the everyday in opposition to drama necessarily reduce their applicability to a very narrow range of films, and the traction of such definitions is questionable even when applied to films that are considered representative. Instead, through detailed case studies of Bresson's *Money* (1983) and Haneke's *The Seventh Continent* (1989), I present an alternative approach that allows for a more nuanced appreciation of everyday aesthetics, allowing for the consideration of films which do not treat the everyday as strictly positive. These films are unsettling precisely for their lack of authorial guidance on how to respond to horrific narrative events; film style is pared back in such a way that moments of violence are afforded the same aesthetic weight as the representation of ordinary and mundane routines.

Chapter 4 expands on both the aesthetic tendency to refuse guidance in relation to depictions of violence, and the need in the critical discourse that surrounds extreme cinema to impose coherence on violent representation. Where the films in Chapter 3 stylistically equate moments of extreme violence with the banal, Chapter 4 considers films in which the intrusion of violence into the everyday is marked as a definite rupture. Catherine Breillat's *Fat Girl* (2001) and Bruno Dumont's *Twentynine Palms* (2003) establish familiar patterns and worlds, only to break them with paroxysms of violence in their final minutes. Disoriented by these seemingly illegible shifts, critical and scholarly responses tend to interpret them in terms of a shift in genre, or dismiss them as an authorial misstep. Unpacking these responses, and considering issues of authorship, genre and aesthetics, I argue that it is the films' broader orienting structures that pave the way for disturbing affect. This chapter considers the ways in which Breillat and Dumont's films involve us in ways that go 'beyond genre' (Thomas 2000: 9), establishing what I call proximate and alienating structures congruent with the theoretical distinctions between positive and negative conceptions of the everyday.

In contrast to the films examined in chapters 2 to 4, which tend to culminate in events of violence, and end abruptly thereafter, Chapter 5 turns to films which draw attention to the endurance of the everyday, and the persistence of violence within it. Gaspar Noé's *I Stand Alone* (1998) and Markus Schleinzer's *Michael* (2011) offer insight into what a return to the everyday following violent disruption might look like. What is potentially most troubling about these films is their implication that violence and the everyday are perhaps not mutually exclusive. In varying ways, both films depict violence as something that might be absorbed into the very fabric of the everyday. Drawing on theoretical conceptions of everyday time as both measured and perpetual, eventful and repetitious, this chapter argues that these films frustrate our desire for coherence by making explicit the fallacy of the narratives we construct to make the everyday meaningful. I claim that by undermining our attempts to understand onscreen violence with legible meaning, these films extend their potency by calling attention to the meaning we project on life outside the cinema; *I Stand Alone* and *Michael* challenge us to question just what is at stake in acknowledging the everyday as indeterminate.

If chapters 2 to 5 interrogate the ways we might conceive of the everyday and its relation to violent disruption – at times seemingly radically separate, at others almost indistinguishable – the conclusion turns to Gaspar Noé's *Irreversible* (2002), a film that has us look back at the everyday through the lens of violence, provoking an experience of the everyday as lost. Pulling together the various threads of argument made throughout, the conclusion is itself an attempt to look back at the significance of the aesthetic tendency outlined, and what it might have to say about the nature of the everyday we live in.

NOTES

1. Taken from Catherine Breillat's *Fat Girl*, Markus Schleinzer's *Michael*, Chantal Akerman's *Jeanne Dielman* and Michael Haneke's *The Seventh Continent* respectively.
2. Of course, this is a highly contested term. According to Catherine Fowler, the concept of European cinema is a critical construct, for 'outside the critical field there is no "European cinema"' (2002: 1). Likewise, Thomas Elsaesser argues that any examination of European cinema 'should start with the statement that there is no such thing as European cinema, and that yes, European cinema exists, and has existed since the beginning of cinema' (2005: 13). The term has typically been used to describe national cinemas in Europe. Considering the rise in transnational productions, however, I find it feasible to use the term European cinema in regard to these films. This is not to suggest European cinema is a monolithic entity, but to acknowledge the diverse range of funding bodies that go into single projects. Luisa Rivi explains that as European nations have their own established industries and styles, the rise in transnational production hints at the tension between visions of Europe as individual and global (2007: 39–41).
3. While predominantly focused on European art cinema, Asbjørn Grønstad's study of the 'unwatchable' also finds examples of 'a cinematic tradition that aims sometimes to question, other times to destroy the sensation of visual pleasure and even to violate the moral or emotional consciousness of the viewer' (2012: 6) beyond the bounds of Europe. Examples include Jane Campion's *In the Cut* (2003), Tsai Ming-Liang's *The Wayward Cloud* (2005) and Carlos Reygadas' *Battle in Heaven* (2005). Similarly, Nikolaj Lübecker's study of the 'feel-bad' film includes examples of American cinema like Brian DePalma's *Redacted* (2007) and Harmony Korine's *Trash Humpers* (2009). Beyond the scope of this study, but worth considering also, is the rise of Asian extreme cinema, associated with filmmakers including Takashi Miike, Park Chan-wook and Fukasaku Kinji.
4. See Coulthard, 'Interrogating the Obscene' (2011: 180–91).
5. See Grønstad, 'Bodies, Landscapes, and the Tropology of Inertia', in *Screening the Unwatchable* (2012: 57–83).
6. See Lübecker's chapter 'Unease' in *The Feel-Bad Film* (2015: 60–103).
7. The view that authenticity is to be found by breaking with the routine forms a significant strand in Western philosophy. Karl Jasper's conception of the 'limit situation' describes moments in which man is confronted with the limits of his being, resulting in a kind of existential revelation. Georges Bataille's (1986) writing on eroticism similarly privileges the need for convulsive rupture as a means to authentic experience. Further, Sheringham notes a tendency in European modernism to find the authentic in the event, noting the privilege paid to 'epiphanies' in the work of James Joyce, and the 'moments of being' described by Virginia Woolf (2006: 27). An extension of this line of thinking sees not just disruption but violence itself as possessing a revelatory quality. Jean-Luc Nancy's *The Ground of the Image* (2005), for example, posits that there is a tendency in Western thought that associates violence with authenticity. Nikolaj Lübecker (2007) furthers this claim, pointing to examples spanning from Christian martyrdom to contemporary French thinkers such as Georges Sorel, Alexandre Kojève, Georges Bataille, Maurice Blanchot and several others.

8. This notion of a 'hidden totality' is something I return to throughout this book. By invoking the term here I refer to Lukács' sense of totality as a kind of unifying essence, as articulated in *The Theory of the Novel*: 'Totality of being is possible only where everything is already homogenous before it has been contained by forms; where forms are not a constraint but only the becoming conscious, the coming to the surface of everything that had been lying dormant as a vague longing in the innermost depths of that which had to be given form; where knowledge is virtue and virtue is happiness, where beauty is the meaning of the world made visible' (1971: 34). Importantly, what Lukács means in using the term 'totality' appears to change over the course of his works. For a comprehensive overview of the nuances of his use of 'totality', see Jay, *Marxism and Totality* (1984: 81–127).
9. The term 'affect' has a long and complex history in film studies. For simplification, however, we might think of this history in two key strands: cognitive approaches to affect, and phenomenological approaches. A cognitive approach to film affect examines the text as stimulus for perceptual and cognitive response. For examples of cognitive approaches to affect and viewer response, see Carroll's chapter, 'Affect and the Moving Image', in *The Philosophy of Motion Pictures* (2008: 147–91) and Bordwell's chapter, 'The Viewer's Activity', in *Narration in the Fiction Film* (1986: 29–47). By contrast, a phenomenological approach to film affect attempts to account for the filmgoer's experience as 'embodied' by redressing the gap between objective phenomena and subjective consciousness. For examples of phenomenological approaches to film affect, see Sobchack's *Carnal Thoughts: Embodiment and Moving Image Culture* (2004) and Steven Shaviro's *The Cinematic Body* (1993). For more general coverage on the term affect and its history in film studies, see Plantinga's chapter, 'Emotion and Affect', in Livingston and Plantinga's edited collection *The Routledge Companion to Philosophy and Film* (2009a: 86–96), Gregg and Seigworth's edited collection *The Affect Theory Reader* (2010) and Brinkema's chapter, 'Film Theory's Absent Center', in *The Forms of the Affects* (2014: 26–46).
10. Beugnet's *Cinema and Sensation: French Film and the Art of Transgression* (2007), for instance, draws on Deleuzian theory, phenomenology and Bataille's writing on transgression to explore the way certain films privilege corporeal sensation over traditional character and narrative, facilitating more proximate relations with the text. Horeck and Kendall's edited collection, *The New Extremism in Cinema: From France to Europe*, is similarly concerned with the affective potential of extreme cinema, 'perhaps not surprisingly, given the emphasis on the nature of embodied spectatorial response' generated through its reception (2011: 6). In another example, Lübecker's *The Feel-Bad Film* (2015), while predominantly concerned with an ethical approach to film, is very much interested in the various ways in which films have the capacity to elicit negative emotions.
11. Theories about the way in which viewers engage with cinema texts are complex and multifarious. Influential approaches over the history of spectatorship theorisation have included screen theory, cognitive film theory and reception studies. Screen theory examines dynamics of desire, pleasure, illusion and ideology often through the lens of psychoanalysis. For examples of screen theory, see Baudry's 'Ideological Effects of the Basic Apparatus' (1986: 286–98), Metz's *The Imaginary Signifier: Psychoanalysis and the Cinema* (1982) and Mulvey's chapter, 'Visual Pleasure and Narrative Cinema', in *Visual and Other Pleasures* (1989: 14–26). Cognitive film theory is interested in the processes by which we might identify or otherwise engage with onscreen characters via affective responses such as sympathy and empathy. For examples of cognitive film theory, see Bordwell's *Narration in the Fiction Film* (1986) and *Making Meaning: Inference and*

Rhetoric in the Interpretation of Cinema (1989), Plantinga and Smith's edited collection *Passionate Views: Film, Cognition and Emotion* (1999) and Carroll's *The Philosophy of Motion Pictures* (2008). Finally, reception studies undertakes case studies of specific audiences, privileging contextual factors such as advertising, reviews and focus group research as the locus of meaning-making. For examples of reception studies, see Altman's edited collection *Sound Theory Sound Practice* (1992) and Staiger's *Perverse Spectators: The Practices of Film Reception* (2000). For a more in-depth overview of theoretical approaches to spectatorship, see Plantinga's chapter 'Spectatorship' (2009b: 249–59), Coplan's chapter 'Empathy and Character Engagement' (2009: 97–110) and Wojcik's 'Spectatorship and Audience Research' (2007: 538–44).

12. The approach I take privileges films as objects for interpretation and reflection. As John Gibbs and Douglas Pye argue, appealing to what is discernibly apparent in a film acknowledges the text as both a stable object that can be consulted to substantiate or invalidate claims, and grounds for 'sharable experience' (2005: 4). Likewise, V. F. Perkins acknowledges that while a viewer's involvement with a film is inevitably influenced by individual traits and experiences, critical judgement 'depends on a predictability of *dominant* responses' (1993: 141). While affect is important in articulating what it means to be disturbed by film and how this might happen, this book is primarily interested in the screen aesthetics that I argue are employed in attempting to evoke this kind of experience.

CHAPTER 2

Everyday Moments

Salò or the 120 Days of Sodom/Salò o le 120 giornate di Sodoma (Pasolini 1975), *Come and See/ Idi i smotri* (Klimov 1985)

When Pier Paolo Pasolini's *Salò or the 120 Days of Sodom* – an updated adaptation of de Sade's literary masterwork of torture and degradation – screened at the New York Film Festival in 1977, Vincent Canby was unimpressed. For Canby, Pasolini's relocation of the novel's characters from their eighteenth-century castle in Southern Germany to the fall of the Mussolini regime was an intellectual and political statement that works 'on paper', but cannot be realised onscreen with the same theoretical distance. Writing for *The New York Times*, Canby states:

> For all of Mr Pasolini's desire to make 'Salo' an abstract statement, one cannot look at the images of people being scalped, whipped, gouged, slashed, covered with excrement and sometimes eating it and react abstractly unless one shares the director's obsessions. Far from being the 'agonized scream of total despair' the New York Film Festival calls the film, it is a demonstration of nearly absolute impotency, if there is such a thing. Ideas get lost in a spectacle of such immediate reality and cruelty. (1977a: 11)

A week later, Canby continued his attack in another article, comparing the film's simulated perversions to the 'simulated … intelligence that attempts to justify this sort of sensational (sometimes vomit-inducing) imagery as a political statement' (1977b: 32). And just one year earlier, Canby had published a more general lamentation at the state of excessive violence in cinema both at home and abroad in an article entitled 'Explicit Violence Overwhelms Every Other Value on Screen'. In this piece (written before Canby had seen *Salò*) Pasolini's 'attempt to make political point out of scenes of systematized rape, castration and other forms of amputation, disembowelment, defecation, and such' only warrants one sentence amid a catalogue of grizzly moments in then-recent films including *Taxi Driver* (Scorsese 1976), *In The Realm of the Senses* (Oshima 1976) and *The Last Woman* (Ferreri 1976), among several others. While Canby finds the violence of Schlesinger's *Marathon Man* (1976) acceptable for what he regards to be the film's greater artistry, he laments that in an increasing number of films – 'movies made without any art and with no purpose except to shock' – graphic violence becomes an end in itself (1976: 69). For Canby, this perceived distinction between art with violence, and violence for violence's sake 'is what separates today's violent films from those of earlier decades (the 1930s gangster films) that were in their own times thought to have gone too far' (ibid.: 69).

Readers familiar with James Quandt's scathing attack on extremes in French cinema almost three decades later will already recognise the similar rhetorical stance. His seminal article 'Flesh and Blood, Sex and Violence in Recent French Cinema' would almost echo Canby's criticism, this time directed at Bruno Dumont's explicit *Twentynine Palms* (2003):

> Asked why he set out to disturb his audience in *Twentynine Palms*, Dumont responded: 'Because people are too set in their ways, they are asleep. They have to be woken up ... You can never definitely say you are human, you have to regularly be confronted by something, to remind you that you still have a lot to do as a human being, you have to be awakened.' Awakened, though, to what? What new or important truth does Dumont proffer that his audience needs to be slapped and slammed out of its sleepwalk into apprehending? In his sophistry, Dumont may place himself in the tradition of provocation, from Sade to Rimbaud to Pasolini, but *Twentynine Palms* has none of the power to shock an audience into consciousness evident in the elliptic violence of Bresson's *L'Argent*, the emotional evisceration of Eustache's *The Mother and the Whore*, or the bitter sexuality of Pialat's *A nos amours*. (Quandt 2004)

Finally, lamenting Dumont's film as just one in a large spate of shocking but ultimately vacuous French films, Quandt concludes that the genuine indignation that gave rise to films like *Salò* and Jean Luc Godard's *Weekend* (1967) has been swapped for inauthenticity, 'an aggressiveness that is really a grandiose form of passivity' (2004).

There are a few points of overlap between Canby and Quandt's responses to contemporary examples of boundary-pushing violence onscreen that are worth noting. First is the sense in which both authors find that the immediacy of the violence overwhelms the viewer so that any intended meaning is lost. While acknowledging authorial intention in the employment of graphic violence, Canby and Quandt are both at pains to highlight the respective films' perceived failure in expression of meaning. Second, there is an eagerness to dismiss the new as excessive and separate from earlier, more purposeful examples of violent representation. Whereas for Canby, Pasolini's film effects something very close to 'absolute impotency' – part of a greater trend in cinema which unlike its predecessors privileges violence over meaning – for Quandt, the very same object is regarded as the bastion of genuine political subversion from a long-gone era. Rather it is the *new* new extreme that, in its lack of perceived purpose, equates to a 'grandiose form of passivity'.

The enduring power of films like *Salò* to unsettle suggests that beyond the immediate reactions extreme cinema provokes is the potential for both the accrual of meaning over time, and a more pervasive, enduring kind of affect. This affective dynamic would seem to be implicit in the notion of the extreme itself. As Horeck and Kendall argue (drawing on Frances Ferguson's study of pornography), the very concept of the extreme necessarily involves an element of novelty (2011: 5), and yet it is not a fixed category, for what is considered extreme is endlessly being renewed. However, where Ferguson considers this constant regeneration of what is deemed pornographic to efface the power of its predecessors,[1] for Horeck and Kendall, new extremes in cinema balance this sense of progressive newness with an historical indebtedness. While they invoke Quandt's term, Horeck and Kendall do not suggest that the new extremism is unprecedented, rather they argue that the term new extreme cinema signals a 'bridging position between newness and indebtedness to the past, to a history of transgression and provocation that is renewed and given a visceral immediacy for the present' (2011: 5–6).

While for Horeck and Kendall the focus is on the visceral immediacy of extremes, this chapter seeks to reframe the way we might approach the affective potential of these works by considering the role of the everyday in bridging past and contemporary examples of disturbing cinema. In order to do this, this chapter first outlines what I call a 'discourse of immediacy', that is, the prevalence of a discourse that locates the affective potential of extreme cinema within the immediacy of shock, outrage and disgust, before teasing out what I take to be an equally important strand of more lasting affect – the disturbing. Further, this chapter argues that what remains in many new extreme films as a degree of continuity with extreme films of the past is the central mechanism that throws the everyday and extreme into tension, or what I'm calling 'disturbing aesthetics'. Despite both pre-dating the new extremism and being ostensibly divorced from any sense of the ordinary, this chapter argues that two notoriously disturbing films – Pier Paolo Pasolini's *Salò or the 120 Days of Sodom* (1975) and Elem Klimov's *Come and See* (1985) – both draw upon the everyday for their impact. Further, because both films are firmly located within times of war and trauma, their gestures towards the ordinary are all the more remarkable in their seeming incongruence given the sort of worlds they depict. In articulating the everyday as a factor in bridging past and present extremes, it is not my intention to suggest that this connection is seamless. Rather I mean to investigate the role of the everyday as a significant point of continuity, as a means of exploring the relationship between the extreme as something that is both indebted to a history of transgression, and something that is necessarily revived.

DISCOURSE OF IMMEDIACY

At its best an evocation of displeasure, at its worst a physically damaging experience, the affective dimension of extreme cinema, new and old, has come to be a defining feature. As Horeck and Kendall state of the new extremism, beyond challenging content, 'it is first and foremost the uncompromising and highly self-reflexive appeal to the spectator that marks out' its singularity (2011: 1). Incidences of audience unrest such as 'fainting, vomiting and mass walkouts' have formed a consistent emphasis in the commentary surrounding new extreme cinema, concerned with its affective potential to shock and confront (ibid.: 1). This is most obvious in press coverage of the films; Quandt's employment of terms like 'slapped' and 'slammed' to describe a film's address to spectators is not unusual. Reviews of new extreme films, both negative and positive, frequently describe a film's address in terms of physical assault. For example, in his review for *Time of the Wolf* (Haneke 2003) Peter Bradshaw describes Haneke's cinema as 'wound-searchingly, bone-scrapingly real: extreme cinema without anaesthetic'. Jonathan Romney of *The Guardian* describes Gaspar Noé's *I Stand Alone* (1998) as 'cinematic terrorism – a nail-bomb directed at the audience' (1999: 8). Similarly, Angelique Chrisafis' defence of Noé's *Irreversible* for *The Guardian* describes the confronting nature of the film in corporeal terms:

> Vomit trickled up into my mouth about four minutes into watching Alex anally raped on a piss-coated subway floor ... You feel – from her face and his contortions – the organs ripping, leaking across the floor ... I felt my unknown neighbours in the cinema seats beside me knarling [sic] their tongues, twisting in their chairs, desperate to leave, but desperate to carry on with the film ... As a viewing experience, it was like being grabbed by the hair and having your face forced fast into a bowl of freezing water, while you sat there unable to breath [sic], limbs flailing, attempting to cover your face. (2002: 8)

Chrisafis's description is one of multisensory assault, her language evocative not only of her own sense of violation, but the perceptible unease of those around her. Her vocabulary absorbs the visceral immediacy of the onscreen assault, with its ripping, leaking, gnarling, twisting, grabbing, forcing and flailing, suggesting both the aggressive stance of the artwork towards the spectator, and a distressing lack of distance between the two. Notably, the terms used to illustrate the affective response of Chrisafis and those around her almost exclusively connote suddenness. These adjectives point not to a pervasive sense of discomfort, but a forceful and urgent jolt to one's experience.

This tendency in response to representations of extreme violence in film is not unique to examples of new extreme cinema. Elza Adamowicz describes the 'rhetorical excesses' common in the positive reception of Luis Buñuel and Salvador Dalí's collaboration *An Andalusian Dog* (1929). Notorious for its opening moments in which a woman's eye is suddenly sliced open with a straight razor, the film prompted several critics to respond in a capricious style, their vocabulary seemingly absorbed from the film (2010: 18). Describing the vitriolic response of British critics to *Straw Dogs* in 1971, Charles Barr observes that Peckinpah's film 'is only one of a line of more or less distinguished films whose violent or gruesome elements have produced an overall critical response which can be termed hysterical' (1972: 26). And the decade following saw widespread moral panic surrounding the 'video nasties' in Britain, the reactionary press coverage of which Martin Barker describes as 'pure adjectival horror' (qtd in Petley 1984: 351).

The rhetoric employed in criticism to describe the affective quality of the new extreme films, and indeed a long history of violent cinema, is concerned with capturing one's immediate reaction. The recurrent allusion to assault pertains to a physical and cognitive involvement that is characterised by a sense of temporal urgency. While this discourse of immediacy is common, at times critics' responses also refer to a sense of discomfort that lingers beyond the immediate shock of extreme moments. Roger Ebert's account of his experience watching Lars von Trier's *Antichrist* (2009) is indicative, noting the tension between moments of extremity and a more subtle and enduring feeling of unease. Ebert's first account of the film described the audience experience at the Cannes premiere. 'We looked in disbelief. There were piteous groans. Sometimes a voice would cry out, "No!" At certain moments there was nervous laughter. When it was all over, we staggered up the aisles' (Ebert 2009a). Coming to grips with his response a few days later, Ebert asserts, 'Enough time has passed since I saw the film for me to process my visceral reaction, and take a few steps back.' Referring to *Antichrist*'s moments of jolting violence, he states: 'Its images are a fork in the eye', and yet, Ebert admits, it is a film that 'will not leave me alone' (Ebert 2009b).

Andrew O'Hehir's review of Claire Denis' *Trouble Every Day* (2001) for *Salon* is similarly balanced between a description of the immediate sense of visceral horror afforded by the film and a more nuanced and enduring kind of unease. O'Hehir (2002) describes the experience of Denis' film as akin to 'biting into what looks like a juicy, delicious plum on a hot summer day and coming away with a mouth full of rotten pulp and living worms'. Ultimately ambivalent about the film, he concludes, 'It's the kind of movie that stays in your head a long time, nibbling at your cerebral cortex' (ibid.: 2002). Ebert and O'Hehir's experiences are closer approximations of the kind of affect this chapter attempts to grasp. While for the most part, discourse surrounding the new extreme films privileges the undeniable abrupt shock of (often unexpected) moments of graphic violence, in employing the term 'disturbing' I am really trying to capture the crucial tension between the immediate, shocking and eventful, and its aftermath.

Moreover, the tendency to privilege a sense of immediacy when accounting for extreme cinema's affective qualities is not relegated to popular criticism. Scholarly studies of extreme cinema often locate the affective, ethical, political potential of extreme cinema in its moments of rupture. Grønstad's study of 'the unwatchable', for example, invokes the notorious moment from *An Andalusian Dog*, describing the confronting nature of new extreme films as metaphorically performing 'razorblade gestures'. With this term he refers to instances of provocation pertaining to 'the emotional, psychic, and ethical slicing open of the gaze of the spectator' (2012: 6). Palmer's interrogation of the French *cinéma du corps* likewise describes 'a mode of cinema invoking a sensory experience at times threateningly, violently attuned to corporeal processes' (61). Michael Goddard likewise attributes the subversive potential of works such as Phillipe Grandrieux's *A New Life* (2002) and Ulrich Seidl's *Import/Export* (2007) to 'their resort to violence, monstrosity and extreme sensations' (2011: 83).

In highlighting this tendency towards a discourse of immediacy in critical and scholarly accounts of the affective potential of new extreme cinema, it is not my intention to diminish their value. Rather I mean to point out that the emphasis on moments of sudden rupture as the locus of affect is a significant point of continuity in the way extremes in violent cinema have been framed over time. If Horeck and Kendall's project looks at the bridge between new and past transgression in terms of visceral immediacy, the remainder of this chapter calls for an approach that might help us get closer to bridging the past and contemporary in terms of a more enduring affect. This is not to negate the importance of the extreme; instead, I argue that the longevity of disturbing affect is intimately linked to the immediate and eventful – evinced in the relationship between the extreme and the everyday which are thrown into tension. We might think of it as a distinction between the suddenness of the 'lapel grabbing kineticism' that Jonathan Romney (2004) evokes in response to Noé's cinema, and the more insidious sustained affect signalled by O'Hehir of Denis' film 'nibbling at your cerebral cortex'.

TOWARDS THE EVERYDAY

Part of my desire to reframe the way extreme cinema has been approached – to interrogate the role its extremeness has to play in generating disturbing affect – comes from what I take to be a kinship between the kind of meaning-blocking manoeuvres employed in many works of cinematic extremism and indeed a much broader history of art. I have described this aesthetic as a means of extending a film's affective quality through the hindering of our desire for hermeneutic closure – effectively a lack of aesthetic containment. In the films examined in the remainder of this chapter, such a dynamic is evinced in a manipulation of the regimen of looking, through the potential for certain sights to be destructive to the beholder, but also through a calculated withholding of traumatic spectacle. Martin Harries' analysis of Orazio Gentileschi's painting *Lot and His Daughters* (see Figure 2.1) is illustrative of the kind of dynamic at work.

Gentileschi's image is overtly expressive of the sense in which an artwork might gesture beyond itself. The painting depicts a biblical scene after the destruction of Sodom and Gomorrah, Lot's wife already having been petrified for disobeying the angels' commandment and looking backwards at the

Figure 2.1: Orazio Gentileschi, *Lot and His Daughters*, c. 1622 (digital image courtesy of the Getty's Open Content Program).

devastation. In Gentileschi's painting, an intoxicated Lot rests his head in the lap of one of his daughters, whose outstretched arm points to something out of frame. Heeding this gesture, his other daughter, too, stares into the distance. The daughters' look references their mother's forbidden gaze, internalising this prohibition into its framing; as Harries asserts, 'the painting is at once alluring and built around the deliberate frustration of the spectator's sight' (2007: 10). By imploring the viewer to look beyond the frame, Gentileschi establishes a paradoxical dynamic: 'The daughter's gesture is a sort of imperative, but the painting's central device makes it impossible for any spectator to obey this imperative' (ibid.: 11).

The pointed absence of the spectacle that Lot's daughters signal towards provides a useful analogy for the way in which the films examined in this chapter incorporate disturbing aesthetics. Pasolini's *Salò* and Klimov's *Come and See* foreground the damaging potential in looking at traumatic spectacle, and yet, for all the emphasis placed on bearing witness to extremes, in the moments where the everyday does intrude, both films crucially play with the distinction between seeing and not seeing.

SALÒ

> And it came to pass, when they had brought them forth abroad, that he said, Escape for thy life; look not behind thee, neither stay thou in all the plain; escape to the mountain, lest thou be consumed ... Then the LORD rained upon Sodom and upon Gomorrah brimstone and fire from the LORD out of heaven; and he overthrew those cities, and all the plain, and all the inhabitants of the cities, and that which grew upon the ground. But his wife looked back from behind him, and she became a pillar of salt. (*The Bible: Authorised King James Version*, Gen. 19:17–26)

Released in the mid-1970s, *Salò* remains a notorious example of cinematic provocation and is still regarded as one of the most disturbing films of all time. Adapted from Sade's bloodthirsty manuscript of the late eighteenth century, Pasolini's adaptation modernises the scenario, transporting the four libertine protagonists and their adolescent victims to the final days of Mussolini's Italy. The film plays out like the grimmest of fairy tales. The Duke, The President, The Bishop and The Magistrate stage a perverse theatre, having captured the surrounding countryside's finest boys and girls and spirited them away to a remote palace. Four of the boys are designated soldiers, another four appear to be the libertines' dedicated sex abettors and the remaining boys and girls form a mostly nondescript group of victims. The libertines' daughters become servants, and four more women are employed, three of whom will recount erotic stories while the other accompanies their narration on the piano. The narrative is divided into four chapters: 'Antechamber of hell', 'Circle of obsessions', 'Circle of shit' and 'Circle of blood', each chapter escalating the perversions and violence onscreen.

Vincent Canby was not alone in his revulsion at *Salò*'s graphic content. Judy Klemesrud, also writing for *The New York Times*, noted the audience response upon its screening at the New York Film Festival: 'At the Sunday night screening, gagging noises from spectators were heard during some of the scenes, and about two dozen members of the largely male audience walked out' (1977: 43). Joy Gould Boyum of the *Wall Street Journal* describes feeling conflicted in how to offer commentary on *Salò*, questioning how the critic is to remain unbiased when faced with 'the kind of active repugnance this work is capable of arousing' (1977: 15). Boyum goes on to suggest that *Salò*'s 'assault' is too extreme to make an appreciation of its artistry even possible.

Reviewing for *The Guardian*, Derek Malcolm acknowledges the film's provocation while praising its artistry: 'every single passage in this long and perfectly structured and decorated film attacks our sensibilities until they are broken off and crushed. The film even denies pessimism, since that after all is some kind of feeling' (1977: 10). For Malcolm, *Salò* is a film in which 'no defence mechanisms are allowed' (ibid.: 10). Still controversial in 2009 (thirty-four years after its release), David Church (2009) analysed the cultural reception of *Salò* as a 'sick film' in online discussion boards, noting that the film is consistently high on fan lists of 'sickest/most extreme/most brutal' films.

There is no question as to *Salò*'s transgressive representation. The film's young characters are raped, forced to eat excrement, physically and psychologically tortured, and finally murdered. It is unsurprising then that the film's affect is predominantly described in terms of shock and revulsion. While any discussion of the film would be incomplete without considering these aspects, I would like also to turn attention to the often overlooked significance of *Salò*'s more muted moments. Though Pasolini's film is far removed from any sense of ordinariness (the youngsters are literally wrenched from the everyday in the film's opening), this is not to say that there are no ordinary moments within it. While the film's graphic elements are undoubtedly confronting, it is these moments in which the everyday encroaches upon the extreme that prove integral to the film's disturbing quality. That is, *Salò*'s capacity to gesture beyond itself is, in part, attributable to the tension between its understated moments and its scenes of brutality.

Salò is a film obsessed with looking: almost every scene revolves around characters watching, inspecting or else presenting themselves for the gaze of others. Early in the film, fascist officers round up the landscape's best-looking adolescents, escorting them to the palace for detailed inspections. Several scenes are spent having boys and girls auditioned before their captors, the

EVERYDAY MOMENTS 25

Figure 2.2: Watching characters watching in *Salò*.

libertines pausing to highlight their merits and deformities as one might shop for fruit.

The room we become most familiar with, the Orgy room, is a massive space serving as both stage and auditorium for the madams' storytelling. The grandiosity of this room is accentuated in wide shots which form highly choreographed images, conscious of their own fabrication and beauty. Boys and girls litter the outskirts of the frame in four distinct areas governed by their respective masters, exquisitely posed in arrangements more reminiscent of tableau vivant painting than film (see Figure 2.2). Spectatorship is internalised; much of the film is spent watching the characters watching, as the three madams in turn recount tales that progress from traditional eroticism to grotesque and murderous perversion. In the corner, a pianist accompanies their narratives with renditions of Chopin.

When not listening to erotic tales in the Orgy room, the film's characters dine together in huge banquets, stage grandiose weddings, and participate in perverse games for the libertines' satisfaction. Very rarely are we given characters' private moments; instead, almost every scene features the entire cast, alternating between active participants and passive onlookers to a given scene's events. In one noteworthy instance, boys and girls are arranged in groups around the borders of the frame, waiting to witness the marriage of three of the libertines to their sexual abettors in a bizarre ritual. In a tense but patently ridiculous moment, The Duke dressed in formal female attire berates the observers for not bearing the appropriate joy and enthusiasm. As if in response to try and lighten the mood, the pianist, who has not spoken a single word up until this point, runs from her place in the corner to initiate an impromptu theatrical performance with one of the storytellers, garnering the desired laughter from the audience. Once complete, the performers just as quickly resume their places at the outskirts of the frame so that the wedding may proceed.

For all its oddness, this scene is emblematic of the way Pasolini manipulates the dramatic emphasis within a scene populated by numerous characters, shifting the locus of our (and the characters') look. Such a patterning of vision is evinced several times in the film. In an early banquet scene, our attention is redirected from the libertines ruminating on the nature of evil when a soldier trips a servant to rape her to the amusement of those watching. Moments later, ours and the cast's look is taken up again when The President runs about the room displaying his rear to the various diners, before presenting it for the same soldier to penetrate. Storytelling scenes are similarly punctuated by assorted disruptions, shifting our attention between the macro and the micro.

In part, the expansive nature of *Salò*'s scenes, and Pasolini's handling of these patterns of looking, functions to distance us from any one character. *Salò* is obsessed with looking, but it is a kind of looking that remains at the level of surface. Outward appearance trumps interiority, and no amount of attention to detail promises to yield insight into its characters' often incongruous actions. As Indiana notes, with the entire cast present in most scenes, and a lack of any character development, the film gives the impression, not of individual protagonists 'but rather a generalised, malignant energy field generated between oppressors and victims' (2000: 69).

The film's fascination with and control of vision in combination with its distancing devices, proves integral to its climax. The horrors we have witnessed in the film thus far now culminate with unprecedented explicitness as the remaining victims are tortured and killed. And yet, amid the most graphic representations of violence in the entire film, Pasolini inserts an oddly unassuming moment that is rendered strange by its very ordinariness. I want to consider this sequence in some detail as it is both where the violence reaches its climax, and where the subdued and ordinary encroach, problematising attempts to secure meaning.

In a very rare instance, *Salò*'s final scenes depict events taking place outdoors. From an elevated position inside, libertines take turns to look out into a courtyard where the remaining victims are held naked and captive to be scalped, blinded, branded, raped, hanged and dismembered. Again, the nature of witnessing is brought to the forefront here: as the dignitaries sit smiling and staring through binoculars down at the atrocities below, we are given their point of view. In this sense, the violence they witness is simultaneously seen and not seen; torture is rendered highly visible by the magnification of the binoculars, but it is also highly mediated and aestheticised. The distance between subject and object is emphasised in a clear disjunction between sound and vision; at first the images of torture are accompanied by a distant piano, and later by an ominous ambience, for though we see the captives screaming in agony below, we are removed enough not to hear their cries. As Bondanella observes, this disparity transforms 'the static tableaux and the suffering human beings they contain into abstract objects for aesthetic contemplation' (2009: 429).

Mediated and aestheticised though it might be, the violence in this sequence is hard to bear. In close-up (through the binocular view) we see a boy's tongue cut from his mouth, another's eye is plucked from its socket with a knife, genitals and other body parts are burned with hot pokers and candle flames, and a young woman is scalped. It is worth noting that while critics struggled to reconcile the graphic content with Pasolini's intended message, these moments are not ambiguous. In the very first scene, the libertines meet to sign an agreement, concluding when The Bishop rests his hand on a notebook marked 'Regulations', stating: 'All's good if it's excessive.' In keeping with Sade's work, Pasolini also includes passages in which the libertines' expound their ideology; over dinner, of a drunken evening, and just in general conversation, they wax philosophical about the nature of power and evil with reference to Baudelaire and Nietzsche. The bloodshed in the film's climax forms the logical end point of the libertine's pursuit of excess. Amid the horror of this final sequence, however, is an oddly undramatic but significant moment.

This moment focuses on the pianist (whom we have all but forgotten about by this point) alone in the Orgy room, who abruptly ceases playing her piano and rises. Already dwarfed by the magnitude of the room, her slow walk from one side to the other to leave it emphasises her diminutive figure further. Walking upstairs and through two vacant bedrooms, she opens a window. There is already something odd about this moment. What might easily be an ordinary occurrence, a character walking from one part of the palace to another, or actively searching for its inhabitants, feels strangely off-kilter. Rather than examining the rooms she enters and exits, the pianist walks expressionless to her destination as though drawn there with a quietude that feels disconcertingly pre-ordained. She climbs a chair to sit on the windowsill looking downwards. Her expressionless countenance turns suddenly to shock and gasping, her hand rises to her mouth (see Figure 2.3). Curiously, we are not granted her perspective. Instead, we cut to a wide shot looking in from the next room, the narrow frame of the doorway bordering the narrow frame of the window, as the pianist climbs awkwardly in her high heels to jump to her death.

The pianist's suicide is rendered undramatically with a composed matter-of-factness in contrast to the aesthetic pretension of the torture scenes outdoors. The viewing dynamic has not changed – we are still watching a character watching. However, in contrast to the shots of the libertines viewing

Figure 2.3: Gesturing beyond the frame – the pianist's unrequited gaze in *Salò*.

the horror below, or the prior instances of Pasolini redirecting our attention by shifting the dramatic emphasis of a scene, our perspective is not aligned with the pianist's. Like Lot's wife's forbidden gaze, the pianist's downward glance is obliterating, but similarly, like the dynamic effected in Gentileschi's painting, our vision in this instance is frustrated. The pianist's response implores us to look, but our look is denied. There can be no doubt that her suicide is a response to some horrible sight, but it is a sight to which the audience is not privy, somewhat bizarrely in the midst of a film that does not shy away from violent spectacle. The gap opened by the withholding of her subjective shot is significantly incongruous with the obsessive emphasis on the libertines' perspectives that bookend this moment, and indeed we return, after her death, to the libertines' exploits in the courtyard with unprecedented explicitness. The refusal of a reverse shot here is itself a way of refusing clarity. While we can speculate as to what she sees, there is no defining image to anchor the pianist's gaze, and so meaning cannot be secured.

The analogy I draw between Gentileschi's painting and the unrequited gaze of the pianist might seem to be undermined by the moment's bookending between graphic scenes of torture. Where Lot's daughter's gesture implores us to look at something restricted by the frame, an appeal that cannot be met, it is possible that we have already been granted access to a sense of the pianist's vision through the libertine's binoculars. If we assume that the pianist is looking at the same tortures we have already seen, as might be implied by the scene's placement, perhaps there is simply no need for a reverse shot here. This argument is problematic for two reasons, however. First, even if we could be sure the pianist does look to the courtyard, her look is only momentary, and so the specificity of what she sees remains undefined; the viewer is still left with the impossible task of filling the gap. Second, it is *her* look – a gaze not aestheticised by binoculars – that we do not see. Just as Harries points out that an apparent forgetting of Lot's wife in a number of artistic representations 'hides a more complicated kind of acknowledgment' (2007: 9), so too does the absence of the pianist's point of view.

Adding to the peculiarity of this moment is the fact that we, as spectators, are the only ones privy to the event at all. Violence throughout the film is used theatrically, staged for an audience – in one example, a female victim is forced to eat The Duke's faeces in front of her peers, in another a boy is whipped brutally and a girl is fed food laced with nails during an elaborate exercise whereby all victims are gathered and implored to play-act as dogs. In striking contrast, the pianist's defenestration is a private act; no one is present to witness it, nor is it acknowledged afterwards by any of the characters. Where other instances of violence are witnessed and responded to onscreen, however abhorrently, we alone are left to consider what this gesture means.

Immediately after the pianist's death we return to the torture in the courtyard, the film's brutality reaching its apex. Several more minutes are spent charting the carnage outside, the libertines still alternating between roles as participant and distant observer. As The Magistrate gazes out of the window, a listless soldier, Claudio, sits on the floor nursing his gun as Carl Orff's dark and menacing 'The Joyous Face of Spring'[2] plays on the radio. Shortly afterwards, he changes the station to the more upbeat classical score 'These Foolish Things', that we by now recognise as the film's ironic theme tune. Instantly, the boy adjusts the tone of the scene from the sinister to the cheerful. Claudio asks a fellow soldier if he can dance and the final image is a touching and graceful waltz (see Figure 2.4). 'What's your girlfriend's name?' Claudio asks his colleague. 'Marguerita' he responds, and the pair dance on. The banality of this moment in the context of what we know to be occurring outside is striking. Ironically, Pasolini's darkest film ends on an upbeat and poignant note.

Where Sade's manuscript leaves nothing to the imagination by detailing every event in his 120 days in an obsessive taxonomy, including a list of survivors, Pasolini's film points towards an ending without actually representing it. The forces that signal finality – the sound of approaching planes, the death being meted out in the courtyard – are ultimately retreated from. Instead, Pasolini's film ends on a relatively ordinary scene; focusing on the boys' dancing to the radio inside, the film concludes on the event of least consequence. As Armando Maggi observes, *Salò* lacks a sense of resolution; the film 'cannot have an ending because an ending would allude to a closure, to some sort of cathartic denouement that *Salò* cannot grant' (2009: 337).

Where *Salò*'s status as disturbing has been invariably attributed to its sadism, violence, perversity and seeming disdain for both its characters and

Figure 2.4: Retreat into the ordinary – the final image of *Salò*.

audience, I argue that what might account for the lingering affective discomfort that it instils in its viewers stems from instances in which the everyday is thrown into tension with the extreme through a calculated restriction of our access to it. After this catalogue in physical, psychological and sexual cruelty, and beyond the film's capacity for the immediate affect of shock and revulsion, is the more pervasive and lasting quality of these moments and their implications – the potential for extreme horror to become coloured by the ordinary as a still accessible memory, or resource.

With its emphasis on witnessing witnessing, and its attention to traumatic spectacle, Elem Klimov's *Come and See* has been similarly framed in criticism and scholarship in terms of the immediacy of its affective impact. In a peculiar and momentary gesture towards the everyday, *Come and See* throws the ordinary and the extreme into tension in a way that affords the potential for a more lasting, disturbing affect. The following analysis of *Come and See* further develops my call to reframe discussion of extreme cinema, exploring how the dynamic of looking and not looking, or even looking but not seeing, serves to extend the aesthetic experience beyond the immediate horror of confronting violence.

COME AND SEE

And when he had opened the fourth seal, I heard the voice of the fourth beast say, Come and see. And I looked, and behold a pale horse: and his name that sat on him was Death, and Hell followed with him. (*The Bible: Authorised King James Version*, Rev. 6:7–8)

Elem Klimov's *Come and See* is a harrowing anti-war film of apocalyptic proportions. Set in Second World War Byelorussia, the film follows bright-eyed and hopelessly naïve Florya, a boy in his early teens eager to join the partisans in the battle against the Nazis. Leaving his pleading mother and very young sisters behind, Florya is quickly faced with the reality of wartime and the bounds of human cruelty. Separated from his unit, Florya returns home only to find the Germans have already ravaged the township. The boy then stumbles from one horrific vision to another: a terribly burned but still conscious village elder, the massacre of an entire village, the chilling return of his female companion Glasha after she has been brutally raped, the still gasping but horribly contorted remnants of an auto wreck, and finally, the slaughter of a group of captured German soldiers. Like Pasolini's film, *Come and See*'s grisly spectacles are far removed from any sense of everydayness; these are exceptional, albeit factually inspired, circumstances. However, amid the film's catalogue of horrors, Florya's desperation to cleave to the everyday is a vital, if under-examined, factor in the film's capacity to disturb.

In a similar vein to *Salò*, *Come and See*'s reception often highlighted the film's affective quality in terms of immediacy and physical distress. Philip Strick calls *Come and See* 'an epic of derangement', describing the film's mode of address in terms of 'the strain [it] imposes on the spectator, who has the frequent sensation of being a target for scorn, horror and disgust' (1987: 79–80). Lloyd Michaels comments that while the censors approved, 'audiences then and now seem more likely to be profoundly disturbed by the film's unremitting insistence on the injustice, terror, and grief that are the wages of war' (2008: 213). Likewise, Anna Lawton describes the film as 'taking the viewer through a painful physical experience', by which our 'senses are relentlessly assaulted' (1992: 225).

Come and See's involvement of viewers is tied up in an emphasis on traumatic witnessing. The film opens with Florya and another young boy seemingly larking on the beach. However, as Denise J. Youngblood points out, this notion of innocent play is subverted when we realise the pair are actually robbing graves in search of a gun with which to join the resistance (2007: 194). The boys laugh at the admonishment of Yustin, a feeble village elder, the same man who Florya will later face, burned alive but still cognisant enough to deliver reproval in the style of a cautionary tale: 'Florya! Didn't I warn you? Didn't I tell you not to dig?' This is a truly horrific moment of recognition, and one of many in which Florya is brought face-to-face with his expulsion from normalcy into a world of adult cruelty.

These moments of revelation through abject horror become an integral part of *Come and See*'s structure. Klimov's film seems to bank on these horrific moments, playing out like a series of calls to awakening through the shock of its visuals. Where *Salò* resists giving a clear protagonist with whom to identify, so closely are we aligned with Florya's ordeal that these moments of violence amount to a bid to awaken the spectator to the visceral horrors of war as much as Florya. Indeed, *Come and See*'s ordeal is bound up in its catalogue of dreadful visions, and the corollary desire to be released from them. After his encounter with the burned village elder, for example, Florya buries his head in the mud, one of several instances where he shuts his eyes and covers his ears in an attempt to block out his surroundings.

If Pasolini's *Salò* is fascinated with mediated or framed seeing, then Klimov's film is utterly consumed by it. The young protagonist, faced with horror after horror, appears by the film's end to have aged dramatically, the complete and utter devastation of his experiences inscribed on his face. Like Lot's wife who is petrified by what she has seen, Florya's body too becomes physical testament to psychic trauma. To draw on Harries' theorisation of destructive spectatorship, 'it is as though certain powerful sights force the body to become a too-solid memorial to what the spectator has seen' (2007: 17).

While *Come and See*, like *Salò*, is renowned for its moments of shocking violence, I want to examine a more subdued, though no less unsettling scene that I take to be crucial to a more lasting kind of affective discomfort. Foreshadowing Florya's encounter with a long list of traumatic spectacles is a pivotal moment in which he returns home to an empty village and desperately cleaves to the familiar, denying a growing wealth of evidence that something terrible has occurred. This is a turning point in the film which brings into tension a dynamic between seeing and not seeing, both literally and figuratively, and crucially holds taut the distinction between the everyday and the extreme.

After a paratroop attack that effectively deafens our protagonists, Florya leads Glasha back to his home. The village feels all too quiet; we still share Florya's damaged hearing from the earlier explosions but, even so, there are no signs of its inhabitants. The soundscape here is vital in creating the unsettling absence. The lack of human sounds is eerily accentuated by the sounds that remain. As a Steadicam glides backwards ahead of the approaching Florya and Glasha, we hear distant birds, the wind in the trees, an ominous creaking sound, the now barely perceptible drone that has lingered since the aerial attack, and a new sound – flies, whose incessant buzzing becomes more and more oppressive as the scene continues. Outside Florya's house, the pair stop and the camera pans left, leaving them behind to capture a piece of debris that has caught their attention. It is unclear exactly what the item in the road is – a forlorn piece of clothing, a pillow perhaps – the important thing is its portentous out-of-place-ness.

The house is empty, Florya's sisters' dolls are laid out on the floor, the dining table littered with bread, and a fly-ridden bowl. In denial of the bad signs growing increasingly obvious, Florya clings to the familiar. Inviting Glasha inside, he states calmly, 'They've gone out. Sit down ...They've gone out.' Glasha gives a feeble smile as she enters, suitcase in hand. Finding a still-warm pot of stew, Florya eagerly implores her to share. All of this is coloured with a feeling of quiet tragedy; under more pleasant circumstances we can imagine a very similar scene in which this young man invites this young woman to his family home for a meal, a version of the same events which has the potential to play out in any other way than this one.

While Florya seems unaware of the graveness of this quiet, Glasha, slightly older and no doubt more attune to the realities of war from her time with Kosach, the leader of the partisans, knows better. Kindly, she tries to play the role he has made for her, but cannot feign composure for long, and glancing across the room on her second mouthful of stew, turns away suddenly to vomit. Unsettled now, Florya follows her look and we are given his point of view, a creeping zoom on the girls' dolls lined up on the floor, also crawling with flies. The image is uncanny; ordinary playthings in the unexplained absence of their owners are rendered menacing, as the slow encroachment of the camera seems to articulate Florya's gradual realisation. The soundscape simultaneously builds here to accentuate the moment of recognition; the low drone amplifies, anchoring a high-pitched ringing, the sound of flies escalates, and some animal wails in the distance. In response, Florya clutches his ears with his hands, his face distorting into a grimace, and unable to repress a primal groan he runs from the house.

Glasha stands in the doorway, her face torn between her performance as comforter, lodged in the ordinary, and her knowledge that things are in fact horribly wrong. Her expression twitches, teetering between a smile and sheer terror as though her muscles cannot quite decide the appropriate response. Florya, on the other hand, slips back into denial, the slight flicker of a grin transforming his, by now, familiar catatonic stare. 'I know where they are. Let's go!' The pair run from the house, but in a moment echoing Lot's wife's forbidden glance, Glasha turns to look back, spying a great pile of entangled corpses strewn against the side of the house (see Figures 2.5–2.6). Stifling a scream she runs to catch up with Florya, but a piece of clothing in the mud prompts him too to look backward. It is unclear whether Florya sees the bodies, his family surely among them. Glasha raises her arms out desperately, grabbing him in an attempt to shield him from the vision.

This backwards gaze is not physically obliterating as in the destructive look of *Salò*'s pianist, rather it marks a kind of psychic annihilation for *Come and See*'s protagonists. This is the pair's first encounter with traumatic looking, an event that seems to trigger the catalogue of violent spectacles that follows. In a

Figures 2.5–2.6: Lot's Wife – Glasha looks back in *Come and See*.

film so heavily invested with the transformative power of vision, this scene is significant for its balancing of seeing and not seeing.

Florya is called to awakening here, a call which he ardently resists. With a kind of cognitive dissonance, Florya desperately cleaves to everyday objects and routines, choosing to interpret discrepancies as indexical of slight rather than grave disruptions to the ordinary fabric of things; an empty house signals his family has gone out, a warm pot of stew indicates they have not been long gone and are likely to return soon. The signifiers required to make sense of his surroundings are present but misinterpreted in a failure to acknowledge the intrusion of violence into established and formerly reliable patterns of habit and meaning. We might consider Florya's return home and subsequent denial of calamity as an attempt to reinstate, if not maintain, a stable and consistent everyday in the wake of uncertainty and chaos. If the film's opening reveals that an everyday scene of children at play might really be imbued with violence and the failure to recognise its ramifications (these children after all are not shooting their fingers at one another, but robbing graves for actual guns), then Florya's return home is surely the culmination of these opposing forces.

Ultimately, these are discrete moments in films that are predominantly concerned with excess, violence and immediacy. I do not mean to suggest that there is no distinction to be drawn between the likes of *Salò* and the examples explored in the remainder of this book, in which the everyday is far more prevalent. However, I do want to point out that the kind of dynamic tension between the extreme and everyday still has a significant role to play in some films that seem completely removed from our idea of the ordinary. Indeed, the potential for disturbing affect in the moments examined is reliant on our own sense of the ordinary, rendered conspicuous for its temporary presence in otherwise extraordinary settings.

My discussion of the everyday's importance, even in films that seem paradoxically opposed to it, has sought to articulate the ways in which some works of extreme cinema effectively gesture beyond themselves. I have considered such a dynamic to be observable in the screen aesthetics of the films under scrutiny, arguing that the patterning of the everyday within undeniably extreme works of cinema might evince a kind of affect that is not fully accounted for in the predominant discourse that surrounds extreme films. Where in the films covered in the remaining chapters we look to moments of violence as the 'lightning that illuminates the banal', in the examples explored here it is the very incongruity of everyday moments that compromises our attempts to attribute violence with clear meaning. What we see in more contemporary works of disturbing cinema is a growing emphasis on the everyday in both film style and subject matter. In the following chapter I turn my attention to what too rigid categorisation of the everyday as an aesthetic category might mean, and how the tension between violence and the ordinary can be better approached.

NOTES

1. For Ferguson, the power of pornography is dependent on its sense of newness: 'To feel the force of the pornographic as pornographic is to feel as though one is in its world, not merely viewing it ... If it doesn't feel contemporaneous, it isn't pornography. Pornography brooks no stance involving historical distance' (2004: 152).
2. This movement taken from *Carmina Burana* was no doubt chosen for its association with German Fascism. Composed and performed during the last years of Hitler's Third Reich, *Carmina Burana* has also been criticised as inherently fascist. In *Composers of the Nazi Era: Eight Portraits*, Michael H. Kater describes post-Second World War music critics who labelled Orff's works as 'anti-spiritual, capable of numbing the listener, of delivering him to irrational powers, thus betraying fascistoid traits' (2000: 128).

CHAPTER 3

Everyday Style

Money/L'argent (Bresson 1983), *The Seventh Continent/Der siebente Kontinent* (Haneke 1989)

> My immediate purpose is to place before the world, plainly, succinctly, and without comment, a series of mere household events. (Edgar Allan Poe, *The Black Cat*, 531)

> Be precise in the form, not always in the substance (if you can). (Robert Bresson, *Notes on the Cinematographer*, 119)

Fifteen minutes before the end of Bresson's final film, *Money*, a kindly old woman who has taken in a self-confessed murderer asks him why he has killed – prompting that there must be a reason. Without looking up from the soup she has given him, Yvon responds in monotone, 'I enjoyed it. I took very little and I've spent it all.' This exchange provides an answer, albeit unconvincing, for the central character's slaying of two hoteliers. The event to which he is referring is elided, but we do witness the aftermath in fragments as Yvon walks downstairs with bloodied hands, washes them – the water running red, then clear – folds a pair of bloodstained trousers and empties the hotel's cash drawers. Yvon is visibly unmoved by this act of violence; rather he holds the same rigid facial expression he has worn throughout the film.

This example highlights the central concerns of this chapter – both the undramatic representation of violence, and a confronting deficiency of meaning with which to reconcile it. Both Bresson's *Money* and Haneke's *The Seventh Continent* preclude textual containment through a lack of authorial guidance on how to respond to violent narrative events. This is achieved with a paring back of film style in which moments of violence are afforded the same aesthetic weight as the representation of ordinary and mundane routines. While Chapter 2 dealt with ordinary moments in extraordinary films, this chapter explores another aspect of the spectrum of the everyday in cinema: the concept of the everyday as a film style, and its relationship to the everyday as subject matter. More importantly, it will consider how we might best approach films which bring these two poles into tension. A brief synopsis of both films will help to articulate the central tension between style and content that this chapter explores.

Loosely adapted from Tolstoy's short story 'The Forged Coupon', Bresson's *Money* begins with a schoolboy, Norbert, who asks his parents for an advance on his allowance so that he can repay a loan. Refused, he goes to a classmate for help, and the pair manage to pass a forged bank note at a photography store. Feeling like a fool, the owner resolves to pass on the note and several more that he has mistakenly accepted. The story soon shifts to focus on Yvon Targe, an innocent fuel deliveryman who unwittingly accepts the notes and is arrested when he attempts to use them. Dismissed from his work, Yvon takes a job as a getaway driver for a bank heist for which he is sent to prison. Upon being released, he murders two hoteliers, stealing their money, and then hides out at a country house run by the aforementioned elderly woman. In the film's final four minutes, Yvon will inexplicably murder the elderly woman and her family before walking up to a group of policemen and confessing his crimes in the same affectless monotone. Despite the plot's dramatic events, Bresson's focus remains on the ordinary – money and other goods passing hands from person to person, objects always taking precedence over people. Events are compressed with notable brevity, and the film exercises Bresson's signature direction of subdued or largely inexpressive performances. Consequently, a fast-paced and dramatic plot is rendered in a way that the dramatic force one might expect to be generated by such events is deflated.

In a similar style, Michael Haneke's debut feature *The Seventh Continent* depicts three days over the course of three years in the life of an Austrian family; husband Georg, wife Anna and daughter Eva. Clearly demarcated in three parts, one representing each year from 1987 to 1989, the film is punctuated with the writing of letters to Georg's parents, read in voiceover, giving a superficial overview of, and then updates on, the family (for example, Georg's employment, Anna's inheritance, Eva's health, and so on). In addition, we are shown fragments of the family's lives, some of which show dramatic events (Anna's brother Alexander bursting into tears during an otherwise uneventful dinner, Eva feigning blindness at school) but most of which depict mundane moments (grocery shopping, eating breakfast, the family car slowly progressing through an automated car wash). The facileness of everyday routine is emphasised through repetition; the first two days depicted feature a very similar sequence of extreme close-ups that enumerate details of the family's preparation for work and school with only slight variations to mark the ellipsis. In the film's final part, we may be led to believe the family has decided to emigrate to Australia; this is the reason given to the bank when Anna and Georg withdraw all of their savings, Anna arranges for her brother to take over her share in their joint optometry business and excuses Eva from school, Georg quits his successful engineering job, the family car is sold, and there is talk of cancelling the newspaper subscription. On the final day, however, the family methodically destroys their possessions and commits suicide with an overdose of prescription medication, a decision vaguely outlined in another letter to Georg's parents.

REFRAMING EVERYDAY STYLE

Despite their attention to the banal, to say either film is undramatic would be inaccurate; both *Money* and *The Seventh Continent* include an array of striking plot points. Bresson's film in particular manages to squeeze a bank robbery, a botched prison escape and multiple murders into its 85-minute running time. However, both Bresson and Haneke consistently refrain from the dramatic potential in presenting narrative events, opting instead to focus on everyday objects and patterns. In *Money*, moments that warrant the most dramatic treatment are either elided completely (as in the death of Yvon's daughter, or his later suicide attempt) or displaced onto everyday objects (the acuteness of a slap, for example, is shown in a shot of a woman's hands spilling hot coffee; a prison escape is represented through diegetic sound and a flurry of shadows visible through the gap under a cell door). In *The Seventh Continent*, the destruction of household objects, and the characters that owned them, is represented in the same subdued and precise fragmentary style as the early montages depicting the family's everyday routines. In effect there is a kind of stylistic levelling of events in their being filtered through the everyday.

There is a distinction to be made here between the everyday as subject matter, and the everyday as an aesthetic. These two things are not, of course, mutually exclusive but are in dialogue. In expanding discussion of the everyday in cinema to consider it as an aesthetic, two key works warrant close consideration – Paul Schrader's *Transcendental Style in Film* and Andrew Klevan's *Disclosure of the Everyday: Undramatic Achievement in Narrative Film*. Both Schrader and Klevan conceive of the everyday as a film style distinctive for its de-dramatisation and pared-back expression, which has resonance in the examples cited in this chapter. However, their defining criteria would automatically exclude *Money* and *The Seventh Continent* from being considered under the rubric of an everyday aesthetic. Teasing out the distinctions between undramatic style and dramatic content, I hope to demonstrate why a broader understanding of everyday film style is useful in accounting for conceptions of the everyday that are not so stringently opposed to the dramatic and eventful.

Paul Schrader's study of transcendental style in film, in which the everyday is a key element, examines the style of Bresson, Yasujirô Ozu and Carl Dreyer.[1] For Schrader, 'the everyday celebrates the bare threshold of existence, those banal occurrences which separate the living from the dead, the physical from the material, those occurrences which so many people equate with life itself' (1988: 39). This is not realism, but a stylistic choice by which the world's energy is abated. While real life has its melodramatic instances, everyday film style actively removes any notion of drama. 'Given a selection of inflections, the choice is monotone; a choice of sounds, the choice is silence; a selection of actions, the choice is stillness – there is no question of "reality"' (Schrader 1988: 39). For Schrader, the everyday is a vital step in a greater transcendental style, a style that captures a sense of life's mysteries. Attempts to explain the world through objective realism or subjective interiority threaten to attenuate the transcendental through feeble reasoning. Instead, by paring style back to its bare necessities, filmmakers like Bresson are able to preserve the immanence of the everyday.

Following a similar corpus to Schrader, Andrew Klevan's *Disclosure of the Everyday* examines films including Bresson's *Diary of a Country Priest* (1951), Ozu's *Late Spring* (1949) and Miloš Forman's *Loves of a Blonde* (1967), arguing that films which are undramatic in both style and content have the potential to reveal profundity. Klevan defines his corpus as films that 'organise their narratives around a range of life experiences unavailable to the melodramatic mode ... life experiences based around the routine or repetitive, the apparently banal or mundane, and the uneventful' (2000: 1–2). He builds on this definition by distinguishing between the everyday as undramatic and films that pursue realism, which despite their focus on ordinary relationships and objects are actually structured around the eventful or catastrophic. For Klevan, films pertaining to the everyday are 'not turbulent or unruly but repetitively rigid ... marked by subdued styles dependent on an evenness of tenor' (ibid.: 44). Drawing on Cavell's reading of scepticism (as giving rise to the paradoxical human desire to transform the ordinary in order to feel connected with it), Klevan privileges films which 'genuinely *acknowledge* the everyday; they do not need to *avoid* it or transform it' (ibid.: 30), their achievement being in conveying profundity 'without the assertion of revelation' (ibid.: 207).

In both Klevan and Schrader's definitions of everyday film style, we can see a partiality for a positive reading in which the everyday is a stylistic sensibility that acts as a conduit to the profound or transcendent. This is a quiet and measured everyday in terms of both style and subject matter. Klevan's conception focuses on films that have the capacity to reveal profundity in the ordinary that we often dismiss. Likewise, Schrader's study sees the everyday as a step in film's capacity to reveal the spiritually sacred. Figured in this way, the everyday is crucial in enabling us to access something deeper, a kind of hidden totality; by attending to the ostensibly ordinary and banal, we might discover the profound.

For Klevan, the profundity of the everyday is located in its fundamental humanity. Examining the famous sequence in Vittorio De Sica's *Umberto D* (1952), in which the maid grinds coffee against her pregnant stomach, Klevan argues that we are offered insight into the maid's personal reflection within her private kitchen space. Her quiet gesture to stretch her leg and close the door with her foot is significant; while such a motion is certainly evidence of the habitual, it is simultaneously 'a rescuing of something from the monotony' (2000: 48). In the maid's routine, there is something liberatory; the familiar offers both comfort and space for expression amid repetition, not unlike the poetry and creativity de Certeau famously observed in the footsteps of Paris pedestrians in his essay 'Walking in the City'. In Klevan's corpus, the everyday and its repetitions, though challenging, seem to provide comfort and liberation in their very ordinariness.

Bresson's treatment of the everyday in *Money*, however, is far less congenial, but no less worthy of our attention. There is an honesty and richness to the elderly woman's routines at the country house as she digs potatoes out of the earth, scrubs clothing in a stream and pins washing on the line; the shift in landscape from the bleak city to the Edenic countryside is alone enough to enliven the banality of daily life, and yet these actions are always inflected with the knowledge that she is a thankless martyr to her selfish family. Following her father's dropping of a wine glass from the piano's edge, we see her in the adjacent kitchen as she responds seamlessly, setting down her pile of ironing to pick up a sponge and dustpan. Such a fluid movement speaks less of interruption to daily habits (she need not even change direction from her previous action) as it does to another ingrained repetition, albeit one that condenses a history of familial dysfunction.

Ascribing to a positive conception of the everyday is not in itself problematic. However, I want to argue that the kinds of distinctions made to separate the everyday from the eventful in dominant accounts of everyday film aesthetics are less robust than they at first appear. One of Klevan's key examples of everyday film style, Bresson's *Diary of a Country Priest* (1951), is illustrative of the issues that arise with stringent attempts to quarantine the everyday. Bresson's film follows a young priest who, alienated from his parish, documents his daily struggles and deteriorating health in a journal. Where Klevan dismisses films like *Paisan* (Rossellini 1946) and *My Childhood* (Douglas 1972) for their ostensive interest in the ordinary, arguing that they are in fact organised around limit situations (in this case, extreme poverty), Bresson's *Diary of a Country Priest* is held up as a primary exemplar of the everyday in film style. *Money* and *The Seventh Continent* would also presumably be excluded for their concern with limit situations – respectively the mass murder and suicide of a family. And yet it is arguable that Bresson's *Diary of a Country Priest*, however unemphatic its treatment, also revolves around a limit situation – a young priest's crisis of health and faith is pushed to its limit, resulting in his death.

For Klevan, it is the film's avoidance of melodramatic style in the face of dramatic content that sees its placement as an illustration of everyday style. The priest's death occurs offscreen, a method of restraint Klevan evokes in his argument for the film's qualification as pertaining to the everyday. Instead this event is recounted to us in the form of a letter from a friend who witnessed his final moments, the text narrated over the silhouette of a cross. Immediately prior to this is our final look at the priest, writing in his diary, before it and the pencil he is writing with slip from his hands. He makes an attempt to pick up the pages from the floor but is too weak to do so. For Klevan, this dropping of the diary stands in for the priest's death, illustrated 'not in terms of its suddenness or its finality, but in terms of the priest being unable to continue with the routine things' (2000: 85). This indeed holds true, but the letter that follows undermines the film's claim to the everyday by Klevan's definition. Described in great detail, the priest's bodily deterioration, replete with 'beads of sweat', 'streams of blood' and a desperate request for absolution, suggest a use of language which is not 'rigidly formal' as Klevan argues (ibid.: 85), but a sentimental appeal to the viewer's emotions.

My point here is that what constitutes drama and its opposition to the everyday in film are not mutually exclusive, nor are they easily defined. Indeed, Klevan later concedes that *Diary of a Country Priest* does have melodramatic characteristics and includes considerable instances of crisis, but that our appreciation of the film might be enriched by considering the way in which it tempers these moments (2000: 99 n1). For Klevan, Bresson's film captures the way that crises do not always live up to our dramatic expectations: 'they are not experienced at the heightened level one might anticipate (or hope for, or need)' (ibid.: 83).

In this regard, Lesley Stern's distinctions between the 'quotidian' and the 'histrionic' are a useful point of intervention. For Stern, these terms describe two cinematic tendencies that exist in varying gradations among all films. They are a means to describe film's fundamental interest in both capturing the patterns and nuances of the everyday, and its propensity for the theatrical and exaggerated (2001: 324–5). We might also think about the range between the quotidian and histrionic in terms of film style; Stern expands her terminology to describe stylistic inflation and deflation, whereby inflation refers to an amplification of formal qualities such as camera movement, performance, and so on, and deflation refers to a tempering of style. One can see where such a continuum might allow for a less problematic discussion of *Diary of a Country Priest*'s gradations between the everyday and the melodramatic. Such terms offer a useful vocabulary with which to discuss films like *Money* and

The Seventh Continent which, while containing histrionic elements in terms of narrative, stylistically deflate these moments. With these distinctions in mind, I now want to turn to the ways in which *Money* and *The Seventh Continent* subdue style in the face of dramatic content, and how this is significantly linked to the films' ambiguous treatment of violence and the everyday.

STYLE VERSUS CONTENT IN *MONEY* AND *THE SEVENTH CONTINENT*

Both *Money* and *The Seventh Continent* temper style through subdued performances and fragmented cinematography, and yet such tempering is not just in the service of conveying the everyday as repetitive or banal – these techniques are also utilised to strategically block our access to character interiority. In the case of Bresson's film, character motivations begin transparently enough (Norbert, the schoolboy, needs money to pay a loan, his friend Martial convinces him to pass a forged note, the store owner is humiliated and decides to pass the note on along with some others, and so on), but by the film's violent conclusion, character actions are all but incomprehensible. For Murray Smith, the film's peculiar patterning can be understood in terms of a 'paradoxical pattern of alignment', where our growing proximity to Yvon's story is counterbalanced by our waning access to his subjectivity (1995: 174). Smith attributes this blocking to a range of factors including the film's elliptical editing, a lack of close-ups of characters' faces, inexpressive performances, and Bresson's propensity for fragmenting dramatic actions into shots of body parts and objects instead of faces (ibid.: 175).

Indeed, Bresson is renowned for his characters' flattened performances, employing non-professional casts who, in Brechtian fashion, were to 'report' rather than embody or interpret their roles (Sontag 1994: 184). For Bresson, actors were 'models' to be shaped like automatons through repetition that sought to divorce action from thought (Bresson 1996: 22). However, Smith points out that in *Money*, slight modulations in performance contribute to the film's indeterminacy by frustrating the viewer's need to interpret character motivation.[2] While for the most part Yvon's performance is flattened, Smith highlights subtle instances where this pattern is broken with displays of emotion, the film's inconsistency in this regard both prompting us to infer meaning, while simultaneously withholding it (1995: 180).

As I will demonstrate, *Money*'s largely inexpressive performances, fragmentation of action and increasingly ambiguous character motivation – its precision in form, rather than substance – throw violence into tension with the everyday, leaving us in want of an explanation. Far from being a straightforward tale of cause and effect like its source material,[3] *Money* is like a tightly bound rope of intertwined characters, actions and reactions that frays more and more the closer one draws to its ending. Where *Money* works to gradually divorce meaning from action, however, Haneke's film is consistently explicit in its provision of signifiers that work to conceal rather than clarify character motivation.

Admittedly influenced by Bresson, Haneke's film style bears several similarities including a fragmented framing of events, elliptical editing, a preoccupation with objects, and often-ambiguous character subjectivity. Nowhere is this more evident than *The Seventh Continent* which, like *Money*, is typified by a blocking of viewer access to character interiority. Amos Vogel, frustrated by the film's ambiguity in which 'too much is withheld and for too long' (1996: 75), overstates its fragmented style: 'Much of the time, faces are not shown, or if at all, only partially' (ibid.: 74). While this is certainly true of the film's opening – we are not afforded a clear look at any of our protagonists' faces for over ten minutes – it is by and large inaccurate. *The Seventh Continent* offers an abundance of lingering close-ups of characters, and yet we come no closer to discerning their psychology. Significantly, where *Money* works to gradually divorce meaning from action, Haneke's film is consistently explicit in its provision of signifiers that work to conceal rather than clarify character motivation.

Neither the structuring letters to Georg's parents nor the intermittent fragments of daily life provide any solid explanation for the Schober family's death. Rarely are we afforded even a hint of character psychology; in largely guarded and inexpressive performances similar to Bresson's characters in *Money*, Georg, Anna and Eva are all typified by a refusal to bear interiority. This lack of insight into character psychology is made pointed in rare moments of emotional outburst, reminding us that it is not that these characters are without feelings, only that we are completely denied access to the feelings they possess. For example, in one of the three scenes in which the family car travels through an automated car wash (another structuring repetition), Anna bursts into tears. We see both her anguished face in close-up, and the expressionless responses of Georg and Eva. Eventually, Georg will raise his hand and gently touch her cheek, though this feeble attempt at comfort seems only to emphasise his incomprehension. And while her emotion is clear – Anna is sad – this sadness remains undefined. Thus, while Haneke's employment of facial close-ups may signal emotion, they bring us no closer to discerning character interiority.[4]

Likewise, the film's use of letter writing as a structural device differs from its traditional use as a means of conveying subjectivity. Where films like *Letter from an Unknown Woman* (Ophüls 1948), *The Shawshank Redemption* (Darabont 1994) and *Atonement* (Wright 2007) employ letters to enrich our understanding of character, Haneke's use of letters in *The Seventh Continent* holds us at a distance, providing an accurate but one-dimensional summary of events.[5] From Anna's summary in an early letter: 'As you see, when it gets right down to it, nothing but good news', to Georg's cryptic offering in the final letter: 'I believe that looking at the life we have lived straight in the eye makes any notion of the end easy to accept', little is revealed, their information remaining strictly superficial.

Like a 'money is the root of all evil' explaining away of Bresson's film, it might be tempting to see Georg's statement as an explanation, a simplistic tale of the ostensibly perfect petit-bourgeois family who despair in realising their lives have become as routine and meaningless as their material possessions. This is the interpretation given by Dennis Eugene Russell, who states that the film's central couple 'spent their lives believing what their government and media told them about consumption equating with freedom and happiness', concluding that the Schobers' self-destruction is a direct response to their despair at capitalist imperatives (2010: 45).

Such justifications gesture towards a need to speak for characters in the absence of a coherent explanation. Haneke's film is disturbing precisely because in the wake of the Schober family's suicide, it refuses to define their reasoning. There is no evidence in the film to suggest the family's feelings of betrayal by the government, nor an equation between consumption and happiness; these sweeping generalisations are indicative of the impulsive necessity to fill ambiguity with meaning. Despite the explicit attention to detail through extreme close-up and repetition, any conclusion we might arrive at to explain the Schober family's implosion seems to fall hopelessly short. As Peter J. Schwartz argues of the culminating destruction and suicide, 'there is no facile way to get from here to psychology' (2010: 343).

This sense of the 'unknowable' is manifest in the film's concern with vision, both seeing and not seeing, the most obvious gestures including Anna's career as an optometrist and Eva's feigning blindness.[6] Following the dinner scene in which Alexander breaks down, he, Georg and Anna sit watching television, a multilingual broadcast. For what feels like a long time, we watch the television also, before Alexander says: 'Do you know what Mama said to me a few days before she died? "Sometimes I wonder how it would be if we had a monitor instead of a head where we could see our thoughts."' Haneke then frames the family's passive faces in individual close-ups, illuminated by the blue light of the television; neither Anna nor Georg show any sign of attention, their eyes remaining fixed on the screen. Consequently, these words are enigmatically suspended; it feels as though our chance to know these characters, Alexander's comment offering a way in, is squandered. Haneke deliberately frustrates our desire for understanding; explicit gestures are made towards the characters' interiority, and yet we are consistently denied access.

Despite the film's preoccupation with objects (apparent from the first preparation montage), the *mise-en-scène* is equally unenlightening as to the characters' interiority. Where *mise-en-scène* is typically utilised to extend our understanding of character, *The Seventh Continent* pares this back also. The film's bleak industrial setting and cold colour palette are often compared to Antonioni's *Red Desert* (1964).[7] Schwartz is correct in his assertion that 'the things and the spaces play as much of a role as the people' (2010: 344), and yet only in the sense that these people are like things. Returning to Schrader's conception of the everyday, there seems to be little separating the Schobers from the dead, the physical from the material, and the human element that does separate them is what Haneke is at pains to withhold.

To consider the everyday as style is to go beyond what is represented, and to elucidate the ways a film might embody qualities of the everyday in its aesthetic treatment. If we accept the everyday itself as being fraught with competing and often contradictory impulses, then instead of attempting to quarantine it from the eventful, we might do better to consider its nuances without necessarily reconciling them. For this reason, I argue that *Money* and *The Seventh Continent* are better understood as embodying an indeterminate conception of the everyday, a conception that preserves the tensions that bear its 'fruitful ambivalence' (Sheringham 2006: 30).

While both films could be described in Klevan's terms as 'repetitively rigid' and 'dependent on an evenness of tenor' (2000: 44), this levelling of style is utilised to unsettle our relation to the everyday, rather than illuminate it for us. The films create an unsettling disparity[8] between such an even tenor and histrionic content. This is observable in consistent patterns of framing despite the dramatic weight of what is being depicted. In Haneke's film, the earlier described scene of the family's faces illuminated by the television in a scene of banal after-dinner routine is recalled towards the end of the film as Anna, Eva and Georg sit watching television in the darkness waiting to die. Events are similarly flattened in *Money*, evident in a scene depicting the elderly woman's father playing piano, a wine glass balanced precariously on the instrument's edge. In close-up we watch it teeter and fall, another close-up capturing its shattering on impact. This event is divided in a similar pattern of fragmented action to moments of violence ranging from the aforementioned slap to the film's final mass murder. Despite the vast difference in narrative weighting between a smashed glass and the murder of a family, Bresson draws a connection through analogous framing and the emphasis placed on inanimate objects over the characters that wield them.[9] Nowhere is the tension between dramatic content and de-dramatised style, and the corollary gap rendered between violence and meaning, more evident than in the films' violent dénouements.

In *The Seventh Continent*, the Schober family's implosion occurs in the third and longest part of the film. The first signal that we have of the interruption to daily routine comes when Georg reminds Anna they must cancel their newspaper subscription. Shortly after, Georg's voiceover is heard reading the final letter to his parents, informing them he has quit his job, an event we see played out underneath his narration. Immediately after, we see tight close-ups at waist level of Georg selecting cuts of meat at what appears to be an upmarket delicatessen. I want to pause on this moment briefly, as it seems to me to be a condensed version of the kind of troubling disparity this film brings to bear. The selection of cold cuts is a mundane enough activity. However, Georg's narration retrospectively lends it a sinister quality. Pointing to pieces of meat, Georg's accompanying voiceover states: 'When you have decided on something you should stick to it.' We do not realise it yet, but the decision to which Georg is referring is the family's resolution to suicide. In this instance, banal decision making in the context of shopping is being equated with the choice between life and death.

Stylistically, the break from or rejection of the daily routine established in the first two parts of the film is hardly framed as a dramatic culmination. The family's death is conveyed with the same monotonous tenor as the preceding events. Like the fragmented treatment of the family's daily habits, the destruction of their possessions is equally mechanised. Beginning with the smashing of a bookshelf, Georg pauses, observing, 'I think the only way we'll make it is if we go about it systematically.' The annihilation of the household and its inhabitants in part three lacks the dramatic treatment we would expect, resulting in an unnerving discrepancy between style and content. Where earlier montages documented the objects and the hands that operated them (radio alarm clock, curtains, toothbrushes, coffee and tea percolator, and the like), the destruction is similarly framed; this time the same hands snap vinyl records, cut up their clothing with scissors, tear apart books and flush Georg and Anna's life savings down the toilet (see Figures 3.1–3.4).

After the methodical and dispassionate destruction of their possessions, Georg and Eva sit side-by-side in the darkness, illuminated only by the television – Jennifer Rush gives a rendition of 'The Power of Love', in which they seem only mildly interested. After a moment, Anna enters expressionless holding a glass and sits beside Eva, who tiredly leans into her mother. In a rare display of affection, Anna places her arm around her. We cut to the television, positioned off-kilter amid the debris. In the following shot, Eva drinks from the glass of poison. 'It tastes bitter,' the child says, handing it back. Shortly after, Eva's death is indexically revealed through a series of fragments, extreme close-ups reminiscent of the earlier preparation montages that documented the family's getting ready. This time Meatloaf sings on the television, and we see the now-empty glass, the child's lifeless outstretched arm, a syringe. The repetition of framing through fragments links this event to the banality of everyday tasks, the child's body now relegated to the status of object. Georg's hand turns off the television, cutting off our soundtrack.

In the most tragic part of the film, Haneke resists allowing the film's style

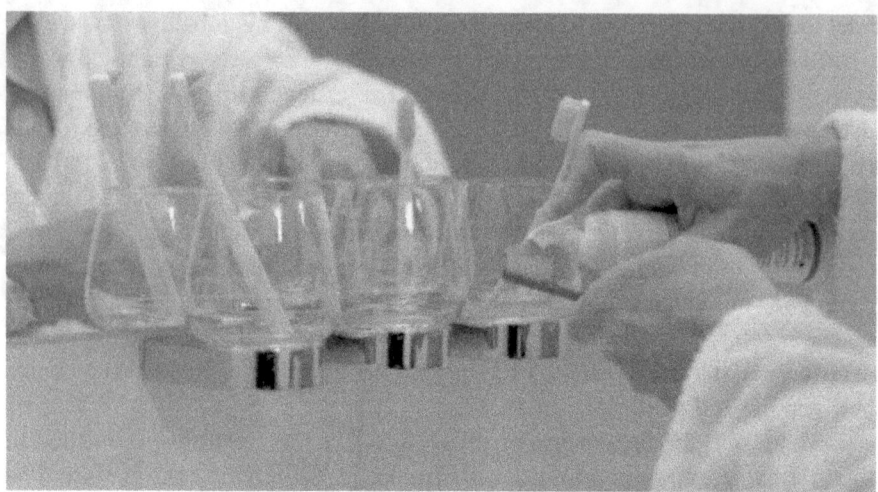

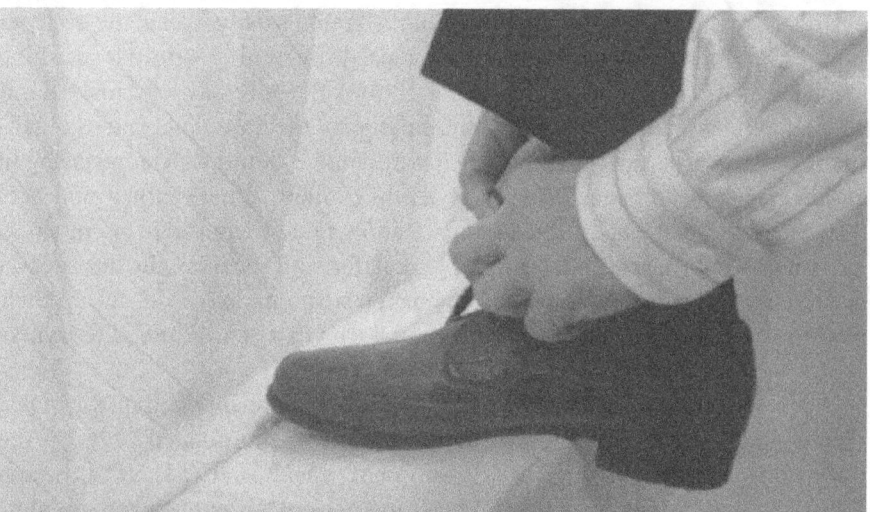

Figures 3.1–3.2: Fragments of everyday banality in *The Seventh Continent*.

to carry the weight of the content – the death of a child. Thus, a histrionic plot point is stylistically deflated. Instead of non-diegetic music to emphasise emotion, we are given (perhaps mockingly) live music broadcasting: emotive appeals for mass consumption. This draws attention to both the absence of music specifically tailored for the event onscreen and the inadequacy of its substitute. The use of music here, failing both to move the diegetic audience and to account for the weight of what we are seeing,[10] highlights how easily manipulated we are by the conventional use of emotive music. Furthermore, Meatloaf's power ballad 'Piece of the Action', which plays over the montage

EVERYDAY STYLE   49

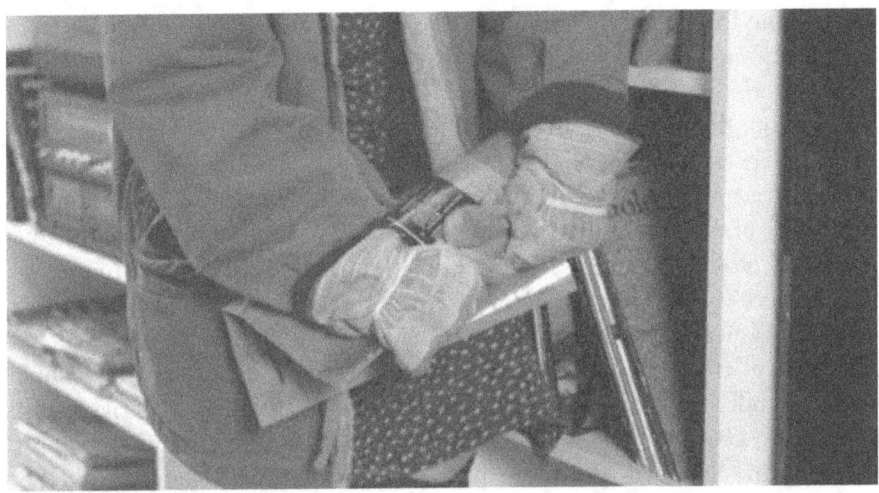

Figures 3.3–3.4: Analogous framing – fragments of self-destruction.

of Eva's death (significantly about a man's frustration at working towards a better future that never appears), gestures towards the feebleness of clear-cut explanations that would draw a straight line between alienating repetition and collective suicide.

This technique of drawing the spectator's attention to a site marked by an absence, by something that is missing, is also evident in the actors' performances. After downing her own fatal dose of sleeping pills, Anna is overcome by anguish and in a distressing image sobs over her daughter's limp body as though trying to wrest it back to life. Anna's affection and then outburst are striking for they call attention to the emotion that has been lacking from the family's implosion thus far. Yet, like other emotive moments in the film (Alexander's breakdown, Anna's crying in the car wash, Eva's tears at the smashing of the fish tank), this is also left unexplored. Haneke resists providing the answers, offering no guidance on how to respond to what we see.

The Seventh Continent draws the viewer in with the desire to understand the interiority of the protagonists; the humanity that separates them from the routines they enact. However, close attention to objects and faces fails to provide the answers we seek. Attempts to decipher the Schober family's actions are blocked; Haneke resists providing explanation, withholding from us a pacifying sense of ethical and moral orientation. Further, the film's tragic dénouement is rendered with a kind of stylistic indifference. Despite the striking shift in content, Haneke refuses to afford it the dramatic address we might expect. Treating the Schobers' death as equivocal to their chores, Haneke – like Poe in his introduction to *The Black Cat* – gives the impression that from beginning to end he is placing before us 'plainly, succinctly, and without comment, a series of mere household events'.

Money similarly deflates the drama of its violent conclusion, Yvon's murder of a family. The fragmentation of actions, privileging of objects over people and use of offscreen space continue the film's previous tenor in spite of the dramatic shift in the weight of its narrative content. In the dark of night, guided by a lantern, Yvon prises open the door to the family home with an axe. Like the previous murder of the hoteliers, his journey through the house is represented in fragments; shots trained on Yvon's torso, as he opens doors and moves from room to room, are followed by a close-up of feet at a bedroom door as occupants get up to investigate. The only sounds we hear are diegetic, conveying the physical qualities of objects; the creak of the wooden door as it gives way, Yvon's shoes on the tiled and then timber floor. Perhaps most alarming, however, is the response of the family dog, which alternates between barking and whining as it runs through the house discovering the dead. The relegation of violence to offscreen space is emphasised as the dog runs first down the empty stairs discovering its master, only to run back up the stairs which are now obstructed by the two corpses of the couple whose feet we had seen only seconds before. The rhythm of this elliptical exchange between open and obstructed gives the violence a horrible efficiency.

Unnaturally positioned though the couple are, the only evidence of brutality comes with Yvon's bloodstained trousers as he casually moves down the stairs. There is a chilling matter-of-factness to this shot; our dreadful recognition of the events in progress seems in conflict with the camera's sober indifference. Indeed, the entire scene has a mechanical impetus; Yvon's implacable advancement from room to room is in contrast to the dog's frantic scamper as it follows in his wake, powerless to stop him. This dreadful recognition is then played out onscreen as the dog runs panting into the woman's room only to stop in the doorway, finding Yvon already there. Its tongue retracts into its mouth as though in realisation, a motion which is rhythmically matched with a shot of the woman's head rising to gaze at Yvon. Her death is prefaced by Yvon's question, 'Where's the money?' before he raises the axe with machine-like rigidity.

'Where's the money?': for Kent Jones, 'the whole sequence – the whole *film* – contracts into these blunt words' (1999: 83). I am inclined to agree, and yet only in the sense that the whole of *Citizen Kane* contracts into the word 'Rosebud'. By this stage in Bresson's film the meaning of money seems divorced from the object, a kind of empty cipher. Where early in the film the transaction of money precipitated a clear chain of cause and effect, by the end of the film its fetishistic value seems to have outstripped its use value. If Yvon is truly driven by a want of money, it seems odd that he does not give the woman longer to reply, or try any other means to coax the answer out of her before swinging the axe. My goal here is not to decipher Yvon's actions, only to point to a troubling ambiguity that they, and Bresson's aesthetic treatment of them, raise.

Again violence occurs offscreen, with the elderly woman's murder signalled by an upturned lamp and the resultant blood spatter on the bedroom wallpaper (see Figures 3.5–3.6). We linger on this image for a few seconds before the light expires, and for several seconds more on the still-visible blood spatter in the darkness. Like Haneke's indexical display of objects to disclose Eva's death, Bresson's foregrounding of everyday objects in lieu of direct representation of violent acts imbues them with an evidentiary significance; red water, spilled coffee, bloodied trousers and broken lamps become the index of violent interactions. Ordinary objects are tasked with bearing the weight of human conflict and cruelty.

The film ends abruptly after this final murder, Yvon taking a drink at a café before confessing his crimes in monotone to a group of policemen. Where Tolstoy's story documents the profound change in the woman's killer, turning to the Bible and transforming the lives of those around him through his saintly influence, Bresson offers no such catharsis. Like the camera's indifference to the brutal murder of the film's most sympathetic character, the curtness of the film's closing moments feels at odds with the event's weight, effectively denying us the dramatic treatment that, in Klevan's words, 'one might anticipate (or hope for, or need)' (2000: 83). That Yvon should kill the only person who has shown him genuine kindness, and to whom in the scene immediately preceding this one he had shown kindness in return, is tragic. However, like the collective suicide in *The Seventh Continent*, Bresson's deflated style refuses to both acknowledge this tragedy and guide our response.

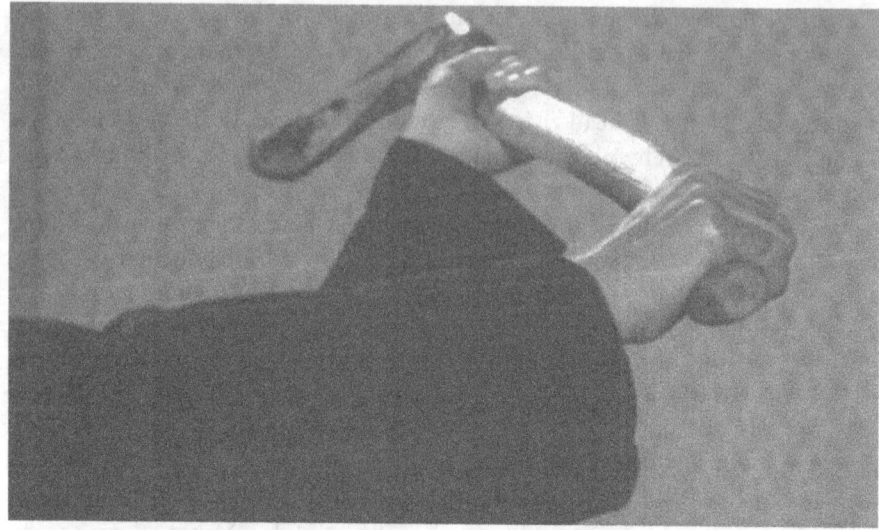

Figures 3.5–3.6: Broken lamps and bloodied walls – violence is displaced onto everyday objects in *Money*.

EVERYDAY STYLE AND THE 'FRUITFUL AMBIVALENCE' OF THE ORDINARY

Earlier in this chapter I argued that while Klevan's approach to everyday aesthetics has been helpful when analysing positive conceptions, it is ultimately limiting. My call for a broader approach to everyday film style is not just in the interest of expanding its parameters to examine a wider body of films, it is also an attempt to circumvent a value system which privileges positive conceptions over indeterminate ones, and, implicitly, narrative coherence over opaqueness. My concern arises out of Klevan's steadfast exclusion of films which literalise the repetitions of the everyday in ways that draw attention to them as repetitions, a criterion that *The Seventh Continent*'s morning preparation montages and recurring car wash scenes would certainly be in breach of.

In a comparable example, Klevan dismisses Chantal Akerman's *Jeanne Dielman* (1975) from his tautology of everyday style, for 'it exploits the possibilities of visual assertion' (2000: 207). *Jeanne Dielman* is Akerman's compulsive stare at the mundane life of a widowed housewife as she cares for her teenage son and goes about her day-to-day business. In static long takes we watch her go about her daily tasks – cooking, cleaning, washing, babysitting, running errands and prostituting herself. Towards the film's end, Jeanne murders a client and yet this clear break with monotony is stylistically treated as though it were another household chore. Akerman describes the even tenor of Jeanne's daily life: 'When she bangs the glass on the table and you think the milk might spill, that's as dramatic as the murder'[11] (qtd in Margulies 1996: 65). For Klevan, real-time, literal depictions of household chores are emphatic and obsessive, in opposition to the unemphatic, undramatic repetition of the priest's journal in Bresson's *Diary of a Country Priest*. Klevan's distinction here is between the 'repetitious' and 'relentless'; his corpus resists films that invoke the literal, concentrating on those that 'engage with aspects of the everyday without remorselessly displaying them' (2000: 207).

The 'relentless' and 'remorseless' display of everyday patterns is indicative of a privileging of understated style; Klevan reads literalness as affording 'undue emphasis' (ibid.: 207). My issue with this reading is linked to my dissatisfaction with an exclusively positive account of the everyday. *Jeanne Dielman* and *The Seventh Continent* certainly use repetition and, respectively, duration and fragmentation to portray the everyday as alienating (in more subtle ways, *Money* does this also), which is of course at odds with a Cavellian treatment. Again, rather than a wholesale exclusion of the film, I find employing Stern's notion of a spectrum of the everyday helpful in animating the nuances of the everyday. In regard to *Jeanne Dielman*, Stern speaks of an inflation of cinematic codes. From Seyrig's controlled performance, to the static wide shots and subdued colour palette, Stern argues that the film employs 'an incipiently histrionic propensity' through the conflation of its formal elements (2001: 330). In contrast to Klevan's dichotomy, Stern's assessment allows for a discussion of the nuances in style and content that, crucially to the films in this chapter, are pitched in opposition. Like *The Seventh Continent*, *Jeanne Dielman* uses repetitive patterning to call attention to the monotony of the protagonist's days, and yet if such a calling to attention or stylistic inflation is occurring in terms of mundane events, this is notably paired with its opposite – a stylistic deflation of dramatic events, leading to an evenness of tenor.

In *Jeanne Dielman* and *The Seventh Continent*, these stylistic devices are used to impart to the viewer the weight of habit upon the protagonists. Akerman's Dielman and Haneke's Schober family seem oppressed by the routines that dehumanise them. Repetition is alienating; the characters' rote performance of tasks likens them to the objects they wield. Margulies highlights this problem in the tension between conceiving of the everyday as potentially utopian humanist ideal and mechanised site of alienation. On the one hand, we consider the positive aspects of everyday life to be creative gestures that resist absorption into the repetitious. On the other, attempts to represent the everyday tend towards literal representation either through an intensification of style or thematic concern with the repetitive and banal. For Margulies, the everyday 'stands, then, both for material reality and for the impossibility to fully account for it' (1996: 26).

It seems to me that implicit in the aversion to literal, emphatic representations of the everyday is a tendency to characterise such representations as negative. If the profundity of the everyday is to be discovered in the subtle and nuanced – in the private moment of a maid grinding coffee in a kitchen, or in the habitual rather than 'remorseless' repetitions of a priest writing in his journal, for instance – then it would suggest that, in contrast, films that exploit 'the possibilities of visual assertion' are stripped of the potential to evoke a hidden totality. If films like *The Seventh Continent* or *Jeanne Dielman* render the everyday extreme by calling attention to its repetitions as alienating and mechanical, then we might assume that the everyday has been stripped of the creative human impulse that affords it meaning. I want to argue, however, that this would be a premature conclusion to draw.

Considered in this way, Yvon's mass murder at the end of *Money* or the Schobers' collective suicide in *The Seventh Continent* would be fundamentally empty gestures. Judging these films as ideologically opposed to the everyday would be to regard them as conclusive tales of cause and effect in which the monotony of the everyday becomes the definitive catalyst for violence. According to Klevan's everyday style, the revelation of profundity arises out of an attention to the patterns and repetitions of daily life, rather than their aesthetic emphasis. While in these terms the films considered in this chapter would not 'acknowledge' the everyday but transform it via what he perceives to be unwarranted emphasis, the everyday portrayed is not simply negative, denying the everyday's immanence. Rather, it is through their motif gesturing towards and then blocking of character interiority that they taunt us with the prospect of a unifying explanation for seemingly incongruous actions.

For this reason, I argue that these films are better understood as conveying an indeterminate conception of the everyday, one that maintains the tensions that afford it 'its fruitful ambivalence' (Sheringham 2006: 30). This is not to suggest that works that privilege ambiguity are of more value than those that do not. Rather, I mean to assert that the lack of closure that these films provide through their indistinct treatment of the everyday is both integral to their disturbing quality and reason for a broader treatment of everyday film aesthetics. The calculated ambiguity in these films is precisely what allows for an everyday that is not foreclosed as negative. Crucially, these are not worlds stripped of their profundity, caught in meaningless circuits of dehumanising tasks. The everyday's hidden totality is equally present and, while tauntingly close, we are not granted access to it.

These negative conceptions of the everyday, do of course find their expression in some films. In Chapter 4 I will argue that Bruno Dumont's *Twentynine Palms* presents us with an everyday where the very possibility for transformation or self-realisation is unavailable. Another notable example is Ulrich Seidl's *Dog Days* (2001). Seidl's film depicts fragments of life in suburban Austria, comprising of an array of unpleasant characters including but not limited to: a grossly overweight pensioner who drowns out his neighbours' domestic disputes with a stationary lawn mower; an estranged married couple still living together after their child's death; a mentally handicapped woman who spends her days hitchhiking with strangers and infuriating them with inappropriate questions and memorised television jingles; a middle-aged woman enamoured with an abusive gangster who humiliates her in alcohol-fuelled spectacles of misogyny; and an insecure hoodlum who physically and mentally assaults his girlfriend. The film provides little, if any, glimpse of a liberating possibility for these people, the everyday overwhelmingly bound by frustration and the cruelty of others. Where *Money*'s elderly woman and *The Seventh Continent*'s Alex at least provide us with glimpses of the world's potential for human kindness and community, *Dog Days* by contrast seems to revel in a punitive parade of repugnant individuals.

Both *Money* and *The Seventh Continent* end without offering sufficient meaning with which to reconcile their final acts of violence. *The Seventh Continent* concludes with the death of Georg. Lying on the bed beside his already deceased wife and daughter, he stares vacantly into the television screen, which now displays static. Against the sound of the television's failed transmission, fragments of preceding moments of the film are interspersed (close-ups – the car wash, faces, objects, transactions, and so on) in what might be flashbacks. If we are to interpret this collision of images as Georg's memories, this might be a glimpse into character interiority, and yet even so, they provide us with no new information or insight. Rather than accruing meaning through montage, these images remain independent fragments. Our final image is a close-up of the television's white noise. No longer contextualised in the diegetic television's frame, the teeming mass of black-and-white particles overwhelms the screen – an image that is paradoxically both something and nothing. Haneke holds this static for an inordinately long time before cutting to black, and a brief epilogue of text outlining events that followed. Describing Georg's parents' disbelief at the prospect of the family's suicide, prompting a homicide investigation, the film's epilogue underlines both the absence of coherent explanation for the Schobers' deaths, and the frustrated need to contain events through the attribution of meaning, a dynamic that applies to the film itself in its troubling lack of resolution.

Bresson's *Money* similarly seems to acknowledge this frustrated desire for closure. Immediately after Yvon's forthright admission of murder to the police, a crowd gathers to watch as he is escorted out of the café. In the film's final shot, Bresson's camera is positioned to peer over the shoulders of the silhouetted onlookers as they stare at the procession of officers and the handcuffed Yvon. Notably, the onscreen observers' heads do not turn to follow as the group walk by. Instead, long after these characters have left the frame – approximately ten seconds in fact – the crowd continues to stare through the open doorway as if in wait of something more (see Figure 3.7). Their gaze, and our own, is unreciprocated, however, as the screen cuts to black. In *Money*'s final shot, the viewer's desire for, and the film's denial of, coherence and closure is played out onscreen.

Central to my argument throughout this book is the idea that disturbing aesthetics are observable in a preclusion of textual containment, promoting an experience of the text as extended through the opening of a gap between violence and meaning in a variety of ways. In this chapter I have examined films

Figure 3.7: Textual openness writ large in the final shot of *Money*.

in which textual openness is apparent through both an equivocating of the dramatic and the banal on the level of film style signalling a lack of authorial guidance, and in the denial of subjectivity that would render the characters' turn to violence legible. In Bresson's film, this occurs in the gradual dissociation between action and meaning; the links in the narrative's chain of cause and effect grow ever more tenuous until they seem to dissolve altogether, making Yvon's massacre at the film's end hard to fathom.

In contrast, Haneke's *The Seventh Continent* is explicit in its provision of would-be signifiers as to character subjectivity, yet these only serve to call attention to the film's consistent refusal to clarify meaning. Further, both films pare back style, proceeding with an even tenor regardless of dramatic shifts in content. Extreme acts of violence are thus treated on a par with banal day-to-day activities, in effect creating an unsettling disparity between substance and framing.

Again, despite a detailed focus on two films, there is of course room to expand these observations to a wider context. Myroslav Slaboshpytskyi's *The Tribe*, for instance, features a scene where a deaf adolescent is killed by a reversing truck; unacknowledged by the film's form, we are left to consider the disparity between the significance of a character's death and the film's unresponsive style. Similarly, Yorgos Lanthimos' *Dogtooth* contains an unsettling moment when the central family's eldest daughter braces herself before the bathroom mirror to repeatedly smash her mouth with a rubber-coated dumbbell. In lieu of aesthetic cues, the visceral impact comes in the spattered blood that suddenly coats the mirror. It is my contention that we need a broader approach to analysing everyday aesthetics in cinema, one that is both able to account for varied conceptions of the everyday as well as attend to its fluctuating degrees and nuances. Where *Money* and *The Seventh Continent* create a stylistic parity between the banal and the extreme, the following chapter examines films in which the break with the everyday is acutely registered. Chapter 4 develops this investigation into textual openness and the unsettling lack of authorial guidance in relation to genre and orienting structures in Catherine Breillat's *Fat Girl* and Bruno Dumont's *Twentynine Palms*.

NOTES

1. Published in 1972, Schrader's book was written before the release of Bresson's later films, including *Money*.
2. Eric Rhode notes a similar dynamic in Bresson's films more generally: 'The Naturalism of Bresson's motifs puts an irresistible pressure on us to expect the usual sorts of explanation for behaviour; but Bresson often ignores motives, quite deliberately ... Because of this unresolved pressure, his heroes arouse a considerable unease in me' (1966: 41–2).
3. Tolstoy's 'The Forged Coupon' features many more characters, and actions and

motivations are always made clear. Further, his original story has a second half in which the murderer finds atonement through the Bible and inspires others through his saintly influence. In its adaptation Bresson condenses characters, renders character motivation in the last third of the film opaque through elliptical editing and inexpressive performances, and omits the second half of Tolstoy's narrative, deeming it 'too preachy' (Bresson qtd in Roud 1983: 11). For a detailed comparison between Tolstoy's story and Bresson's adaptation, see Tony Pipolo (2010: 332–5).

4. Ed Gallafent highlights a comparable instance of character interiority being concealed despite the focus and duration afforded them in Hitchcock's *Under Capricorn* (1949). Describing a shot of the character Hattie alone on the balcony, he writes: 'As she appears in the frame, she turns away from the balcony and leans on the window glass, facing into a breeze. Her eyes flutter open, then close as she leans back, exposing herself to the camera as the wind plays across her face and hair. I suggest that the shot offers the paradox of self-exposure (as an image, a woman, a penitent) and privacy, or self-containment; it invokes what Stanley Cavell has called the woman's unknownness' (2005: 74–5). Describing another shot of the same character later in the film: '… the effect of the long take here, and of the concentration of the camera on Hattie, is to expose her to us, to our interpreting eye, but what is exposed is not knowledge but unknownness: we understand that we will not be able to see and that we cannot know. Rather than an offer of privileged access, we might think of the long take here as expressing refusal, a kind of default position that applies when there is an inability to move into the ways of knowing, or offering or experiencing the world. It speaks of Hattie's self, and what we cannot know of it' (ibid.: 75). Similarly, George Toles describes the final shot of *Queen Christina* (Mamoulian 1933) in which Greta Garbo stares out at the ocean after the death of her lover: 'Now, as the narrative ends, the camera gradually closes in on her impassive, wind-stroked face until it fills the screen. Her expression is unreadable, and our steadily enlarging view of it oddly forestalls emotional identification even as it strengthens the invitation to probe … In such moments as this one … one of the secrets of cinema time – what it means to "live" in the image – is *almost* revealed to us. Thus we are given a perfect illustration of Jorge Luis Borges's definition of the aesthetic phenomenon: "this imminence of a revelation which does not occur"' (2001: 31–2).

5. Eric Rhode notes a similar dynamic in Bresson's *Diary of a Country Priest*, a film in which 'everything is shown, yet nothing is explained' (1966: 36). Bresson's film 'opens on a country priest writing in an exercise book, "I see nothing wrong in noting here, day by day, with complete frankness, the very humble and insignificant secrets of a life which is, however, without mystery." This promise is kept; even so, the meaning of this life (and Bresson is Romantic enough to believe that a man's life of any worth is a continual allegory) can only be caught in the opaque final words, "All is Grace." Everything is shown, yet nothing is explained. Why must the country priest destroy himself in pursuit of a vocation beyond his physical resources? Why is he somehow set apart from other men? Questions like these are opened freely, like doors, only to be later slammed in our face' (ibid.: 36).

6. To highlight this further, in the scene where Anna confronts Eva about this lie, she turns off the children's television programme Eva is watching, entitled *Shau Hin und Gehwinn*, roughly *Look Here and Win*. Oliver C. Speck gives an excellent summary of the film's dichotomy of 'blindness and insight'. See Speck (2010: 76–81).

7. See Brunette (2010: 14); Schwartz (2010: 345); Speck (2010: 136–7); Wheatley (2009: 57–8).

8. My use of the term 'disparity' is in reference to the gaps created in these films between

violence and meaning, dramatic content and de-dramatised style, film treatment and viewer expectation. Schrader's discussion of everyday style uses this word slightly differently. For Schrader disparity refers to 'an actual or potential disunity between man and his environment which culminates in a decisive action'. It is 'an inciting incident' which 'casts suspicion on the nonemotional everyday' (42). For example, in Bresson's films this occurs through the repetition of action – 'If it is "realism," why is the action doubled, and if it isn't realism, why this obsession with details?' – and through the evocation of something 'Wholly Other within the cold environment, a sense which gradually alienates the main character from his solid position within the everyday' (1988: 71).

9. This equivocating of action is not unique to *Money*. Schrader describes Bresson's tendency across a range of films: 'Bresson has a rigid, predictable style which varies little from film to film, subject to subject. The content has little effect on his form. Bresson applies the same ascetic style to such "appropriate" subjects as the suffering priest in *Diary of a Country Priest* as he does to such "inappropriate" subjects as the ballroom sequences in *Les Dames du Bois de Boulogne* and the love-making sequence in *Une Femme Douce*' (60).

10. Christopher Sharrett compares this use of music to an earlier scene in the film where Eva accompanies Georg to a junkyard to sell the family car. While Eva waits for her father she sees a boat passing in the distance and Alban Berg's violin concerto 'To the Memory of an Angel' can be heard. Sharrett writes: 'This composition could be read as a deliberately deformed paean to late Romanticism, a piece that answers the fragment of a Bach chorale, which Haneke remarks may be seen as the film's anthem. Neither Bach nor Berg are connected to the child's plight, and neither these compositions nor anything else of classical culture are viewed by the world of the film as compensatory' (2006: 11). Of the later scene where 'The Power of Love' plays, Sharrett continues, 'The plaintiveness of the song is never diminished within the scene, but it has no more role than Bach (classical culture) or Berg (modernism) in ameliorating the alienating effects of capitalist civilisation in its late phase' (ibid.: 11).

11. Rachel O. Moore observes a similar equation of everyday disruption and violent eruption in Bresson's *Money*: 'Bresson's cinematography in *L'Argent* is so even, so measured that he can render the slap of a face through the consequent spilling of hot coffee with a violence that is on par with if not greater than the massacre of a family' (2000: 108).

CHAPTER 4

Everyday Structures/ Everyday Language

Fat Girl/À ma soeur! (Breillat 2001), *Twentynine Palms* (Dumont 2003)

> Why does the violence in films like this not only shock critics deeply but knock their critical faculty so far off balance? ... What the critics seem to fear is *contamination*. The director is involved: if we respond, we become involved too. Violence is a vampire bite. (Charles Barr, '*Straw Dogs, A Clockwork Orange* and the Critics', 26)

Released in 2001, Catherine Breillat's *Fat Girl* left many critics confounded. For eighty-one minutes of its eighty-six minute running time, the film is a quiet coming of age story of two teenage sisters. Unexpectedly, however, the film ends with a random act of violence: a bloody axe murder, strangulation and rape. This sudden turn to extremes incited a mixture of bewilderment and frustration in reviewers. Describing Breillat's move here as 'an astounding misstep', Bob Strauss (2001) of the *Los Angeles Daily News* states:

> It's a gratuitously violent ending that comes so far out of nowhere, you can only imagine one of three excuses for it (and none of them good ones). Either Breillat simply couldn't figure out where her movie needed to go ... or she somehow decided that her artistic signature requires strong doses of shocking sensationalism in every movie, whether they belong there or not; or, most probably as well as ludicrously, she's suggesting that all male predation operates on a reductive scale on which there is little space between seductive youthful dissembling, marital indifference and sheer monstrosity.

Katrina Onstad's (2003) review in the *National Post* also expresses frustration at the seemingly illogical rupture in narrative. Describing the moment at which Breillat 'tacks on a five minute ending' that undermines the otherwise careful neorealism of the film, Onstad finds the turn to violence 'frustratingly –

dangerously, even – open ended in meaning', labelling it 'an extreme cop out'. Similarly confused, Carla Meyer's (2001) review in the *San Francisco Chronicle* states that despite being 'undeniably riveting, the scene is so out of step with Breillat's otherwise careful plotting that it comes off as a stunt'. For Peter Bradshaw (2001) of *The Guardian*, the violence constitutes 'a shocking but empty gesture', stating, 'the effect of this grotesque eruption following what had been a very well-observed and well-acted human drama is baffling'. In an ambivalent review, Linda Ruth Williams (2001) for *Sight and Sound* comments on the film's 'flawed brilliance', before broaching the 'tricky issue of the shock ending'. Here, Williams' tone turns cynical, surmising that Breillat's turn to violence may be a last-ditch attempt to maintain her authorial persona as a *provocatrice*: 'Perhaps Breillat, reflecting the mismatch between her reputation for shock and *À ma soeur!*'s hitherto relative sobriety, felt that she needed to do something to up the ante.' Finally, Kirk Honeycutt (2001) of the *Hollywood Reporter* reasons: 'In life, of course, irrational and inexplicable events happen. In film, especially in third acts, such actions betray an artistic laziness.'

These responses call attention to an interesting critical problem that this chapter seeks to explore regarding how sudden and violent disruptions to the everyday are to be interpreted. Where the previous chapter examined films in which the illegibility of violence was elicited through its stylistic equivocation with the ordinary, this chapter examines films in which the intrusion is marked as a definite rupture. Catherine Breillat's *Fat Girl*, and the similarly structured *Twentynine Palms* by Bruno Dumont, establish familiar patterns and worlds, only to break them with unprecedented bursts of violence in their final minutes. Grappling with this seemingly illegible change, critics and scholars often focus on the extremity of the films' climax. However, I argue that it is rather the films' broader orienting structures, congruent with the theoretical distinctions between positive and negative conceptions of the everyday, that pave the way for disturbing aesthetics.

FAT GIRL, *TWENTYNINE PALMS* AND THE CRITICS

A brief synopsis of both films will help to illustrate the structural affinity of the shift from the ordinary to the violent, and better contextualise the films' critical reception. *Fat Girl* depicts a wealthy French family on vacation in a seaside village. Chided throughout for being overweight, Anaïs is younger but worldlier than her slim and beautiful sister, Elena. In the film's first scene, the two wander the woodlands surrounding their villa and Elena challenges Anaïs to see who can pick up a boy first. Soon after, Elena is seduced by a much older, handsome Italian law student named Fernando. Offering Elena an expensive engagement ring and declaring his love, Fernando convinces the reluctant and underage Elena to sleep with him. In the same room, feigning sleep, Anaïs quietly sobs as her sister is deflowered. A visit from Fernando's mother reveals the ring belongs to her, and Elena's illicit tryst is discovered, bringing the holiday to an abrupt end. The long drive home is fraught with tension; Elena is heartbroken and ashamed, her mother furious, and Anaïs upset at being caught in the middle. With a duration of under ninety minutes, we know the film must close soon – perhaps with a reprimand from the girls' father, perhaps a car accident (Mrs Pignot's growing fatigue behind the wheel is emphasised), or maybe the family's circumstances will be left unresolved. Instead, in the final five minutes the narrative is suddenly disrupted by a random act of violence; on a night-time rest at a road stop, an axe-wielding maniac smashes through the car windscreen, striking Elena in the head before strangling her mother. Frozen, Anaïs watches from the back seat. The man backs Anaïs into the woods, forcing her underwear into her mouth and raping[1] her. The film ends the following morning, the police bagging evidence at the crime scene. Two officers escort Anaïs from the woods; 'She says he didn't rape her,' one tells another. Anaïs is quick to add, 'Don't believe me if you don't want to,' before turning to glare just off-centre; the film freezes on this frame for some time before the credits roll.

Similarly structured, Bruno Dumont's *Twentynine Palms* follows an adult couple: emotionally unhinged Katia and her pretentious photographer boyfriend David travel the Californian desert supposedly scouting for locations for his upcoming project. The couple spend the majority of the film alternating between sex and arguments of equal fervour, interrupted only by banal conversation and driving through the sweeping landscape. For the most part the film is slow, repetitive, and establishes a predictable pattern of arguments and reconciliations. However, like Breillat's film, *Twentynine Palms* erupts into violence towards its ending. On another desert drive, thirteen minutes shy of its two-hour running time, the couple's Hummer is rammed by a pick-up truck full of archetypal rednecks who beat David's face with a baseball bat before raping him. Katia is meanwhile stripped naked and forced to watch the brutalisation. Back at their motel, David refuses to seek police help, and bursting from the bathroom screaming, his hair haphazardly cut off, stabs Katia to death. In the film's final shot, a police officer finds David's naked corpse in the desert before wandering into the distance while arguing with a fellow officer over his radio.

Both *Fat Girl* and *Twentynine Palms* were released in the early 2000s, amid the body of work retrospectively known as the new French extremity. Structurally, the films follow a comparable pattern – the majority of the running time is spent tracing the dramas of human relationships in a space away from home, before acts of random violence disrupt the film worlds in the final minutes. Both end with the perfunctory police response to this violence. Likewise, both are the products of provocative French auteurs. There are also, of course, important differences: Breillat's film is set in France, while Dumont leaves the provincial setting of his previous work to shoot in the American desert. Further, *Fat Girl* focuses on adolescents and follows the difficulties of a romantic formation, while *Twentynine Palms* deals with adults who struggle with its maintenance.

Despite these differences, within the films' climactic violence is a comparison worth pursuing. While it is the nature of the new French extremity and its intersecting cousins (*cinéma du corps*, cinema of sensation, the unwatchable, and so on) to feature bursts of violence, very rarely is the shift quite so marked off from the rest of the film. François Ozon's *See the Sea* (1997), for instance, culminates in the offscreen murder of its protagonist, a lonely young mother who has taken in a female backpacker for companionship. Returning home from a business trip, the woman's husband discovers her naked corpse, bound in rope, her head wrapped in plastic. Horrible as her end is, it is not entirely unexpected; the backpacker (played with a disconcerting lack of expression by Marina DeVan) is palpably menacing throughout, her behaviour ranging from brazen rudeness to perverse cruelty. Similarly, Claire Denis' vampire tale *Trouble Every Day* (2001) contrasts the banal with graphic violence, yet this violence is both dispersed throughout and made apparent in the film's promotional materials – the majority featuring variations of an image of Beatrice Dalle, her white dress and pallid features drenched in blood.

In another noteworthy similarity, the accusations of ineptitude and pretension aimed at *Fat Girl*'s violent ending with which I opened this chapter were also launched in reviews of Bruno Dumont's *Twentynine Palms* released two years later. In his article on the new French extremity, Quandt (2004) describes the abrupt shift from banality to bloodshed, concerned that a formerly visionary director had become susceptible to a new fad for empty shock tactics. Where Dumont's prior turns to the extreme were 'incorporated into both a moral vision and a coherent *mise-en-scène*', for Quandt, *Twentynine Palms* is both 'absurd and self-important', and reveals 'a failure of both imagination and morality'.

Quandt's accusation of pretension is indicative of a common critical position. In a critique for *The Denver Post*, Michael Booth (2004) describes Dumont's 'bloviated production notes' before attributing the 'huge, inexplicable explosion of action near the end' to a director who has evidently grown tired of his own movie. Labelling the film a 'Zabriskie Pointless', Lisa Nesselson (2004) of *Variety* similarly describes *Twentynine Palms*' shift to violence in pejorative terms, noting, 'Those Euro crix for whom the pic's existential idiocy may register as exotic will no doubt attempt to imbue the late-arriving events with deeper meaning.' In addition to these accusations of pretension is the charge that such a transition is the product of inept filmmaking; Ty Burr (2004) of *The Boston Globe* deems the ending 'miscalculated and laughable'.

Evident in the negative reviews of both *Fat Girl* and *Twentynine Palms* is an irritation with the inability to understand why the films change in the way they do. The consensus among the critics quoted above appears to be that the shift is illegible in relation to the rest of the film; it is 'gratuitous', 'tacked on', 'out of step', 'baffling', 'inexplicable'. Further, to try to make sense of this violence is to suppose one or more of the following:

1. The director's authorial persona is at odds with the film they have created.
2. The director did not know how to end their film out of incompetence, laziness or gross misjudgement.
3. The director's concern is with pretentious and ultimately empty messages.

Over the course of this chapter I will address all of these suppositions. However, I want to start by addressing how *Fat Girl* and *Twentynine Palms* are to be interpreted in the greater context of their directors' work.

AUTHORIAL PERSONAS

Dumont's films prior to *Twentynine Palms* had combined the extreme and the ordinary (though certainly not to the same degree), finding the sacred in the everyday. Both of his previous features contain moments of hard-core sex and graphic violence amid their otherwise dilatory meditations on human nature and painterly landscapes. The teenage protagonist of *Life of Jesus* (1997) ends an ongoing racial feud when he brutally beats his Arab rival to death. Further, the opening minutes of Dumont's police procedural *Humanity* (1999) contain an unsettlingly explicit close-up of a raped and murdered child's bloodied genitals. Despite these confronting images, Dumont's pared-back style, employment of non-professional actors, and allusion to the spiritual and existential properties of the everyday had, in his first two features, established a stylistic affinity with Robert Bresson. While Dumont was always a provocateur, it is a perceived break with the austere Bressonian positivism of his previous films that Quandt's aforementioned critique finds troublesome. While I agree that the redeeming glimpses of humanity amid the world's violence afforded in Dumont's first two features are indeed absent in *Twentynine Palms*, for reasons I will demonstrate later in this chapter, to regard this as the catalyst for an incoherent *mise-en-scène* is misguided.

As evidenced in the negative reviews cited earlier, Breillat's *Fat Girl* was also subject to such criticism, despite its excess being less of an anomaly in the context of the director's *oeuvre*. Her debut feature *A Real Young Girl* (1976) contains a wealth of transgressive imagery; early in the film, its fourteen-year-old protagonist masturbates with a spoon under the family dining table, and later we are privy to a sexual fantasy in which the man she desires has tethered her to the ground with barbed wire before trying to insert a live earthworm into her vagina. Her later *Junior Size 36* (1988) likewise focuses on a young woman's sexual curiosity. Immediately preceding *Fat Girl*, Breillat's sixth feature, the sexually explicit *Romance* (1999) gained notoriety when it faced censorship issues for its depiction of rape, taboo images of male arousal and unsimulated sex. Her 2004 film *Anatomy of Hell* – a study in the abjection of the female body – is perhaps the most transgressive to date. In this film, a depressed and suicidal woman pays a gay man to watch her where she is 'unwatchable' over four nights in a secluded house. Over the course of their time together, we witness several taboo images; on one evening the woman removes her bloody tampon, places it in a glass of water and implores the man to drink. In another instance, the man takes a long handled garden hoe from outdoors and inserts it into the sleeping woman's anus.

While violence is not uncommon in Breillat's films, more often than not it occurs offscreen, as in the accidental shooting of Jim in *A Real Young Girl*, and Marie's murder of her sleeping boyfriend in *Romance* as she leaves the apartment having turned the gas on. Perhaps the closest we get to the horrific violence that ends *Fat Girl* in Breillat's earlier work is the brutal murder of Frédérique in the ironically titled *Perfect Love* (1996). This film ends abruptly after her boyfriend sodomises her with a broomstick and stabs her to death. However, unlike the violence in *Fat Girl*, this event is known to occur from the beginning. *Perfect Love* opens with a documentary-esque handheld camera recording of the killer as he reconstructs the crime for the investigating police officers. In this sense *Fat Girl*'s unexpected, onscreen axe murder and strangulation marks a departure in Breillat's work.

While I acknowledge that *Fat Girl* and *Twentynine Palms* differ in significant ways compared to both directors' prior works, I do not think we should be so quick to regard change as erroneous. The second and third points regarding claims of ineptitude and pretension are considered in my own analysis of the films later in the chapter. For now, however, I want to signal a general response to these claims. The problems with this line of argument are not the dissatisfaction with the films' perceived disunity, or accusations of pretension and laziness. These are reasonable (though I will argue ultimately misguided) responses to the films' shocking elements. Rather, the problem is that, more often than not, this response prefaces a wholesale dismissal of the films, resorting to a normative understanding of what constitutes 'good' filmmaking, and precluding genuine engagement. Among these negative responses, even those that allow that the violence may on some level be an extension of the directors' concerns employ indignation as an excuse to disengage from pursuing the matter further. An alternative and more constructive lens through which critics and scholars have interpreted the violent shift of both *Twentynine Palms* and *Fat Girl* is the notion of genre.

GENERIC EXPECTATIONS AND GENERIC BREAKS

Taking this sudden change in the nature of both films as a shift in genre has formed another common thread in criticism and scholarship. In specific reference to *Fat Girl*'s violent dénouement, Linda Ruth Williams has asserted, 'This is a moment a little like the switch in *From Dusk Till Dawn*, when a genre shift occurs in the instant which divides frame from frame' (2001: 12). Similarly, J. Hoberman (2001) states that Breillat's film 'is a female coming-of-age film that radically redefines its sentimental genre' when the film's 'classical structure climaxes with a violent shift in rhetoric'. Speaking of *Fat Girl*, and Breillat's later *Anatomy of Hell*, Lisa Coulthard describes the way in which violence shifts the narrative trajectory. In both films, violence becomes the factor 'which, in one scene alone, can redefine a film's genre' (Coulthard 2010a: 66). Martine Beugnet similarly describes *Fat Girl* as playing out 'like a slowed-down, out-of-sync version of a teen movie'[2] (2007: 48), before citing the film's 'sudden switch from teen movie to horror' (ibid.: 49).

Twentynine Palms was received in a similar fashion. David Denby (2004) of *The New Yorker* describes Dumont's subversive project along the same lines as the revisionist Western. Dumont (2004), in turn, considers *Twentynine Palms* an 'experimental horror film' and has signalled his intentions in sabotaging expectation: 'If you look at the way the film starts, the scenery and the actors indicate it's going to be an American-style movie, yet nothing happens ... it's a negation of American cinema, almost a terrorist attack' (qtd in Matheou 2005: 17). Nikolaj Lübecker considers the film both a merging and irritation of familiar frameworks; *Twentynine Palms* is both 'a road movie that goes nowhere, since the lovers return to the same motel every night, and a horror film that will frustrate all thrill-seeking viewers during the first 100 uneventful minutes' (2011a: 238). Similarly, Coulthard argues that the film's conclusion 'radically alters *Twentynine Palms*' trajectory, generic tone, and impact' (2010b: 171). According to Coulthard, its final twenty minutes are 'from a register radically distinct' from the preceding hundred, as its violent conclusion 'propels the film's form away from its art cinematic origins into the realm of horror, cult, and genre cinemas' (ibid.: 172).

For these critics and scholars, a generic shift occurs in an isolatable instant in which our concerns and expectations radically change. Such an assessment involves finding the familiar elements which approximate our orientation on either side of this rupturing moment. And indeed it initially seems intuitive to examine the change occurring in these films through the lens of genre in light of the films' manipulation of expectation. While filmmakers have long played with audience expectation and awareness of genre conventions in the creation of hybrid genres, significantly, neither *Fat Girl* nor *Twentynine Palms* is an example of genre hybridisation. Unlike the werewolf as puberty metaphor that binds the horrific with the ordinary in John Fawcett's *Ginger Snaps* (2000), for example, *Fat Girl*'s genres clash rather than combine.

As Williams (2001: 12) points out in her review of *Fat Girl*, Robert Rodriguez's *From Dusk Till Dawn* (1996) is a comparable example, featuring a dramatic shift in generic expectation with its marked transition from crime film to vampire film. However, there is a notable distinction to be made: in Rodriguez's film this change does not bring with it a dramatic shift in the emotional landscape of the film; unlike *Fat Girl*'s last-minute move from the relatively benign trials of adolescence to a confrontation with a homicidal maniac, *From Dusk Till Dawn*'s world is fraught with danger from the outset, and the change in genre simply sees the source of this threat relocated into a supernatural realm. Additionally, *From Dusk Till Dawn* maintains a darkly comic tone throughout, which works to offset what might otherwise be genuinely unsettling moments. For comedic value, Rodriguez's film goes so far as to self-reflexively acknowledge the absurdity of this shift, as in one character's assertion: 'And I don't want to hear anything about "I don't believe in vampires" because *I* don't believe in vampires, but I believe in my own two eyes, and what *I* saw is fucking vampires!'

On the one hand, we might think of genre and the expectations it entails as a kind of safety net, insulating the viewer's experience by affording particular cues as guidance. Asbjørn Grønstad, for example, invokes the generic cues in torture porn films such as *Saw* (Wan 2004) and *Hostel* (Roth 2005) as having a fortifying quality against genuine discomfort, as 'aesthetic form works to render unpleasurable sensations paradoxically pleasurable' (2012: 16). The animosity levelled by many at *Fat Girl* and *Twentynine Palms* suggests that if we are interpreting the shift in generic terms, then the original genre's fortifying qualities have been radically and unexpectedly disrupted. If we take the majority of *Twentynine Palms* to be a drama about the romantic trials of a dysfunctional couple in the desert, the sudden arrival of a truck full of violent strangers is unlikely to be experienced as a welcome innovation; rather this is apt to be the moment when our 'horizon of expectations' (Jauss 1982: 79) is shattered, as though the rules of the game had been broken.

While genre is a handy frame of reference to reach for in accounting for our experience of these films, it is worth questioning the assumptions we bring about their commitments to genre. As Beugnet points out, while several directors of the cinema of sensation 'often draw on and subvert generic elements, the end result is neither predefined by the narrative or discursive operations of genre' (2007: 125). To feel cheated by the shift these films take is, I suspect, to have overstated their allegiance to generic convention. I want to suggest that in attending to the films' broader structures we are better suited to account for the sudden turns to violence.

ORIENTATION BEYOND GENRE

Outlined above are what I take to be critical misunderstandings of the shifts occurring in *Fat Girl* and *Twentynine Palms*. The kind of disjunct many experience strikes me as akin to George M. Wilson's observations about a perspectival phenomenon when viewing a painting in which the perspective focus is off-centre (1988: 10). Wilson describes the inclination to adjust our position so as to align ourselves with the focal point of the image, to give the impression that we are centred in relation to it. For Wilson, a similar tendency applies to certain films, whereby moments of narration that initially appear incoherent can often be better understood by realigning our perspective. It is this kind of realignment I propose will better equip us to make sense of the rupturing moments of violence in *Fat Girl* and *Twentynine Palms*.

Part of recalibrating our perspective in this instance is to consider the ways in which both films orient us in a broader sense, allowing, as Deborah Thomas puts it, that our expectations for the experience that a film will elicit 'go beyond genre' (2000: 9). While *Fat Girl* and *Twentynine Palms* orientate the viewer in one direction for the greater part of their duration and then suddenly disorientate them in their final minutes, I argue that the films' potential to disturb is not contingent on the shift itself, but rather can be accounted for in the broader patterns of orientation, that is, the worlds we are invited to inhabit and the nature of this invitation (Thomas 2009: 9). By taking this approach in trying to understand the sudden violence of these films, we might, as Wilson puts it, achieve 'a more fortunate perspective' (1988: 11).

Granted, these shifts in our orientation are not, as with Thomas' study, between the comedic and the melodramatic[3] – both films operate primarily within a melodramatic register, but, as I will argue of Breillat's film at least, the shifts seem rather to happen between levels of the melodramatic (the extent to which we interpret the world to be malevolent, and where this malevolence is likely to spring from). I want to argue that the disturbing potential of the films in question is best thought of in the ways they shape the everyday, through the structuring of the film world, and through the role of language to involve or distance us. While the varying functions of language may seem an odd thread to pull, it is by no means arbitrary; both *Fat Girl* and *Twentynine Palms* signal their concern with language – most explicitly in their inclusion of romantic couples who struggle to communicate, but also in more subtle ways. Breillat's film, I argue, develops a register of proximity through its aesthetic treatment of the everyday as indeterminate, in stark contrast to *Twentynine Palms*, which provides a resolutely negative conception while holding us at a distance throughout.

TWENTYNINE PALMS

Early in *Twentynine Palms*, a scene begins with a slow, night-time panning shot of an alleyway repeatedly illuminated by the bright bulb flashes of an offscreen photographer. The distant murmur of (police?) radio can be heard amid the overbearing sound of traffic that dominates throughout the film. Katia's voice then emanates from a place seemingly behind the camera, beginning a brief conversation about the couple's plans for dinner. Coinciding with the end of this exchange we see that the camera has done a full circle, and we are viewing the alleyway a second time. Katia's voice is heard again: 'C'est toujours pareil ce truc-là' ['That thing's always the same'].[4] At this point we cut to a wider shot which provides us with the context necessary to see that the alleyway we have been watching is not a place the characters currently inhabit but a looped panorama playing on a television screen in the couple's motel. Another cut reveals the reverse angle: David is sprawled out in bed transfixed by the screen; Katia sits beside him in a towel painting her nails. 'Mais qu'est-ce que c'est ça?' ['But what is it?'] she asks. David responds: 'Je ne sais pas. Je pense …' ['I don't know. I think …']. And then, reverting to an affected English mid-sentence, 'an art film'. He pauses before matter-of-factly adding, 'It's amazing.'

Unless we are familiar with the source material (Thomas Demand's 2001 video art *Yard*[5]), we could be forgiven for assuming this is a point-of-view shot through David's camera, taking photos while Katia talks to him offscreen. We have, after all, been told in the opening scene that David's purpose for driving to Twentynine Palms is to scout locations, presumably for a video or photography project. Dumont plays a bit of a joke on us here; David is not working as we are led to assume, but lazing in bed. In fact, throughout the film we never see him take any photos or shoot any footage. We do, however, see him twice more in similar scenes, naked, save for a sheet or towel, engrossed by the motel television. More importantly, however, this scene gestures towards the theme of monotonous repetition which will structure the entire film; it reflexively acknowledges itself as part of a larger art film, one that is always the same with its repetitive cycle of explicit sex and pointless quarrels.

My point here is that we should not be so quick to dismiss the frustration and monotony of Dumont's film as apathy or pretension, as it is, in fact, carefully calculated. At the very least, this scene should make us question the seriousness of any perceived pretension. Further, as this analysis will show, the culminating violence which so troubled critics is not the incongruous misstep it has been claimed to be; if we find, as Wilson would say, a 'centred viewpoint', we can see that it arises out of the film's structuring orientation of alienating repetition – acknowledged in this scene, and fundamental to negative conceptions of the everyday.

Twentynine Palms is patterned by alienation and repetition in various ways.

This is perhaps most evident in the film's concern with language as both banal and the stuff of conflict. Lines of dialogue are frequently repeated and the film's central couple are plagued by miscommunication; Katia (played by native Russian Yekaterina Golubeva) speaks French, while David is American, and both have only a cursory grip on the other's language. At numerous points in the film their relationship to each other and the outside world is fraught by a labour to communicate. However, language is just part of a greater vocabulary of replication that patterns the film – symbols of repetition are featured throughout, and the wider structure, until its violent dénouement, consists of scenes of either/or in combination: driving, arguing, reconciling, and having sex.

The first words we hear in *Twentynine Palms* are Japanese, emanating from the Hummer's stereo as the opening chord of a playfully upbeat song (one we will hear several times throughout the film) is strummed and a country music-style guitar twangs into life. The film opens on the road, a broad and busy highway, and we watch David's back as he drives. David indicates, leaning forward to look in his side mirror (an act that seems to require his entire body), letting out a frustrated groan at the traffic. Resigning himself to the present lane, he shuffles, reaching into his pocket and removing a roll of red tape which he proceeds to wrap around the steering wheel (possibly to measure the vehicle's over-steer). He then fidgets with something, CDs perhaps, on the seat beside him, his attention darting back and forth between this distraction and the road ahead. David is introduced as restless and childlike – he groans, shuffles, fumbles and fidgets. A cut takes us to a similarly unflattering first glimpse of Katia, asleep with mouth agape in the back seat. Moments later she is awoken by David's mobile phone, which he fumbles to answer. 'Hello? Hello. I'm driving.' David sighs tiredly, licks his lips and purses them; even the muscles of his face seem impatient. 'I'm driving to Twentynine Palms.'

The opening scene's phone call serves as exposition of the plot – David explains he is going to 'check out the location' – but it is also our introduction to the way language functions as repetitive and banal. We see this again shortly after, when the couple pull over to admire a wind farm. Initially it is obscured by an extensive freight train: we watch its long line of carriages pulse rhythmically over the tracks before the couple approach the dozens of synchronised turbines that litter the horizon. Staring up in awe, David says, 'It's great', and implores Katia to listen to the endless cyclic whir. 'C'est magnifique' ['It's fantastic'], she replies. 'Oui,' ['Yes'], David splutters, taken aback as though her response is inadequate, before adding, 'No, it's perfect.' Where the first scene introduces language as repetitive, this scene, replete with symbols of perpetuity, emphasises its redundancy; the couple's relay of interchangeable adjectives does not advance understanding, it merely replicates.

David and Katia's frequent arguments, the first of which occurs less than ten minutes into the film, are similarly structured by repetition. In the scene immediately following the wind farm, the couple are back in the car driving. Taking David's hand, and speaking softly, Katia asks, 'Pourquoi tu penses?' ['What are you thinking?'].[6] David responds flatly, 'Je pense à rien' ['I'm thinking about nothing']. Katia's voice is still light, but pressing: 'Sì, tu penses quelque chose' ['You're thinking something']. 'Non, rien' ['No, nothing'], David replies. Katia pushes again: 'Ça c'est pas vrai' ['That's not true']. Beginning to lose his patience, David shrugs his shoulders, retorting: 'C'est vrai!' ['It's true!']. Katia's voice is slightly harsher now: 'Mais pourquoi tu me peux pas me dire?' ['But why can't you tell me?']. Exasperated now, David reverts to his native tongue: 'I'm driving. What?' In frustration he throws up the hand she was holding, and lets out a heavy sigh as she pulls away. Looking up at her, he asks, 'Quoi?' ['What?'], but the word drawls out with his annoyance, emphasising his American accent. The scene continues and ends without resolution, David trying repeatedly to coax a response out of Katia, whose features we study in long take, shifting from silent anger to hysterical crying. Like the tautological exchange about the wind farm, this argument is patterned by fruitless repetition.

Michel Chion comments on a similarly repetitive patterning of dialogue – what he refers to as 'parroting' – in Kubrick's *Eyes Wide Shut* (1999). In Kubrick's film, parroting has a variety of functions, but generally gives language a detached presence: 'When we hear the words we can never assume that their meaning is entirely transparent, or that they are clearly concealing some precise meaning that is different from what they say' (Chion 2002: 24). This overt use of repetitive dialogue in *Eyes Wide Shut* contributes to the film's enigmatic tone, characters often repeating the lines of others with a paranoid uncertainty that makes familiar words strange. In this sense, parroting in Kubrick's film often opens language up to the possibility of multiple meanings. Dumont's use of repetitive dialogue in *Twentynine Palms*, by contrast, shuts meaning down. Katia and David's exchanges emphasise language as banal and trivial. When the characters fail to understand each other, it is not indicative of some deeper or vital meaning. Rather, their arguments function like a tennis match: words are served and returned, first in their affirmative terms, then their mirroring negative, corresponding with the film's wider pendulation between disputes and resolutions.

This tennis match pattern of conversation is repeated *par excellence* in a later argument in which David grows increasingly frustrated with Katia's contradictory behaviour. Sitting in a café, Katia declares she is starving, before requesting ice cream instead of a meal. David is further confused when the conversation turns to the subject of a marine sitting at another table, Katia stating that she finds marines attractive but should David ever shave his head like one she would leave him. This mild confusion soon transforms into frustration and anger, however:

> David (referring to Katia's ice cream): 'C'est bon?' ['Is it good?']
> Katia: 'C'est pas bon.' ['It's not good.'] (Pause) 'Mais c'est bon.' ['But it's good.']
> David: 'Ah non. Je ne comprends pas. Hein, tu dis des choses que je ne comprends pas.' ['Ah no. I don't understand. Uh, you say things that I don't understand.']
> Katia: 'Mais il n'y a rien à comprendre.' ['There's nothing to understand.']
> David (dismissive): 'Bon.' ['Fine.']
> Katia: 'Bon.' ['Fine.'] (Pause) 'Tu fais la gueule?' ['Are you sulking?']
> David: 'Non, je ne fais pas la gueule' ['No, I'm not sulking.']
> Katia: 'Ah oui tu fais la gueule.' ['Yes, you are sulking.']
> David, exasperated, bursts into rapid-fire English: You know I'd just like to have our conversations to have some sort of logic to 'em because sometimes you say one thing then you say something else and I have no idea what you're saying, this completely dysfunctional conversation, and I, I don't know –
> Katia smiles: 'Je t'aime.' ['I love you.']
> She laughs softly, disarming him.
> David stares at her, before returning: 'J'ai envie de toi.' ['I want you.']

The scene ends as the couple leave the café, arms around one another, before a cut transports us immediately to a shot of them in the middle of vigorous sex back in their motel room.

Even the gentle words spoken between the couple feel vapid in the context of their predictable and perpetual fighting. 'Est-ce que tu es content de commencer ton repérage?' ['Are you happy to start scouting?'], Katia asks David in a Chinese restaurant. David responds softly and slowly, 'Je suis heureux ... être ici ... avec toi' ['I'm happy ... to be here ... with you'], before looking up at her with puppy-dog eyes several times as though waiting for her approval. Seconds later the couple erupt into argument, language dissolving as Katia quietly seethes in response to David's fleeting glance at another woman. Unable to contain her anger any longer, Katia eventually smashes at the table with her fist in an involuntary gesture of inarticulate rage. Vitriol between the couple is so frequent, and Katia's moods so unpredictable, that moments of calm merely leave us in wait of the next dispute.

I point to these scenes as indicative of both the way the patterning of language (as repetitive – oscillating between positive and negative poles) reflects the greater patterning of the film's structure, but also to indicate that in *Twentynine Palms* it is a frustrating abstraction of communication, obstructive to understanding. In the aforementioned Chinese restaurant scene, we hear a chaotic cacophony of maladroit attempts at one another's languages (this time the broken English of a Chinese waitress is thrown into the mix). I want to suggest that Dumont's repetitions in language gesture towards a negative conception of the everyday as not only repetitive, but inconsequential. The couple's interactions remain superficial and constrained; it seems the creative potential in ostensibly oppressive and predetermined structures as described by Michel de Certeau is patently absent. The repetitions of language in *Twentynine Palms* neither signal something deeper (as in *Eyes Wide Shut*), nor do they advance understanding. Rather, the couple's words give the sense of being trapped in a frustrated and tautological cycle.

As described in negative conceptions of the everyday, the alienating patterns of repetition require transcendence or escape if the authentic is to be accessible, and this too plays out in *Twentynine Palms*' treatment of language as an abstraction that must collapse. Indeed, Dumont's film seems to strive towards the dissolution of language. Notably, the couple's arguments tend to dissolve into silence – Katia fumes silently before bursting into tears, David sulks. Where words constantly trip and fail, effective communication in *Twentynine Palms* seems to occur through the primitive and corporeal – physical aggression and sex. As Dumont has said in interview, 'the couple are regressing precisely in their lack of awareness, of verbal language, everything that we think of as human and civilized – to try and revert to some instinctual state' (qtd in Béar 2008: 277).

This regressive turn away from language is emphasised in the couple's frequent sexual encounters. Where Katia is prone to unpredictable emotional outbursts, often radically disproportionate to any given situation, David seems driven by his body, most obviously in a consistent pursuit of sex. We are encouraged to view him in corporeal terms – his shift in the argument cited above from the language of emotion in Katia's 'I love you', to the bodily 'I want you' is demonstrative. David's corporeality is also strongly associated with the animal. In one scene following an argument, the couple swim in the motel swimming pool; face half immersed in the water, David stalks Katia like a crocodile before initiating fierce sex which culminates in his animal-like orgasmic squeals. The couple's (often aggressive) sex seems to be their only successful means of communicating with one another. Significantly, these scenes tend to culminate in David's primal screams, grunts and howls. In this sense, sex brings the dissolution of language, becoming animal; David and Katia connect on corporeal terms, terms that transcend language.

Beyond these extremes between David's bodily drive and Katia's hysterical emotions, language fails to give us any real insight into their characters; rather their dialogue remains superficial. The expository phone call in the film's opening scene is the closest we get to an insight into the characters' existence outside of their present surroundings, and this remains resolutely surface – David is driving to the desert to scout locations, he will be back in a couple of days. With only the vaguest of references to the world they have left, our understanding of character is strictly limited to what we see and hear in their present tense, and illustrated in the banality and repetition of their conversations this hardly gives us any insight as to who these characters are or what their existence entails outside of their immediate context.

This lack of access to character also impacts the landscape they inhabit. Not afforded a sense of the world they have come from, the desert space remains relatively neutral; it is neither figured as a space of liberating escape, nor does it inspire a longing for home. Where other road movies afford us a clear sense of the homes their characters have left – either through direct representation as in *Badlands* (Malick 1973); subjective flashback as in *Natural Born Killers* (Stone 1994); or at the very least via interactions that deepen our understanding of character relationships as in *Wolf Creek* (McLean 2005) – the world of *Twentynine Palms* feels hermetically sealed by comparison. There is no tension between the space of home and the space of the road – they feel like completely separate worlds. Dumont consistently holds us at a distance, positioning us as observers to the couple's habitual sliding between poles of animosity and tenderness.

Bereft of any genuine warmth or opportunities for attachment to the characters and their world, Dumont estranges us; Katia and David are framed as creatures for our observation, a perception writ large in the repeated extreme long shots that diminish them. Dumont's camera often encourages us to view his characters at great distance, becoming mere shapes in the ecology of magnificent landscapes (see Figure 4.1). While this technique had been seen earlier in *Humanity*, like all of Dumont's authorial tropes, it is exaggerated in *Twentynine Palms*. Coupled with an unnaturally loud soundscape (traffic, sirens, wind, the pairs' footsteps are all noticeably amplified), the film world often overwhelms the characters; evoking the sublime, Dumont's photography renders the couple diminutive against desert landscapes that are simultane-

Figure 4.1: Beautiful and overwhelming – the desert as sublime in *Twentynine Palms*.

ously beautiful and threatening. As Beugnet describes, such a grand contrast in scale produces an eerie effect, transforming 'the desert into the vision of a monstrous entity on whose skin the characters seem to wander' (2007: 105).

Rendering the couple as minutiae against the sublime desert, Dumont presents his characters as trivial in an environment indifferent to them. This sense of alienation is exacerbated by both the couple's growing animosity towards each other, and an increasing antagonism of those around them. As the film progresses, the couple's arguments grow more serious (escalating to the point where David will wrestle Katia to the ground in the middle of a road and beat her), and it becomes apparent that they are capable of destroying each other. The potential threat of the outside world is further emphasised by its hostile inhabitants, ranging from the petulant but benign waitress who snatches the couple's menus from them in the Chinese restaurant, to the truck full of rednecks who assault David and Katia in the film's violent ending.

While the exact nature of this later attack may come as a surprise, Dumont punctuates the film with signals as to the world's enmity; midway through the film, David and Katia's attempt to cross the road without looking is met with the disproportionate aggression of a driver who screams abuse at them; after a heated night-time argument in which David throws Katia out of the motel room, she wanders up and down the stretch of road outside hiding twice from passing cars; on a desert drive the couple are passed by a blue pick-up truck, Katia remarking, 'Tu vois comme on est pas tout seule?' ['You see, we're not alone']; and minutes before they are attacked they will have two encounters with the attackers' vehicle – first, while they are pulled over, it stops in front of them and then speeds off (David laughs but Katia voices her trepidation), then later when the couple's Hummer is stuck on a rocky trail, David spies it in the distance.

The couple are assaulted on what will be their final desert drive together; a white pick-up truck they have spied earlier rams their Hummer at speed, forcing them to a halt. Three men pull David and Katia from the vehicle, one sporting a baseball bat. Katia is stripped naked and forced to watch while David is pushed to the ground and repeatedly beaten in the face with the bat before one of the men rapes him. David is incapacitated throughout; bloody and stunned, his mouth ajar in the sand expels a terrible croaking sound. Reminiscent of David's primal cries in the throes of orgasm, as the rapist climaxes he screams repeatedly, finally bursting into tears. A shot of Katia shows her gasping in rage and horror which gives way to hoarse cries.

The film's eruption of violence sees the culmination of its characters' and world's fundamental drive towards the dissolution of language. The final spasm of violence, David's murder of Katia, occurs in the predictable patterning of anger and calm that has structured the film throughout. After a tender moment in which Katia attempts to comfort David, his face hideously deformed in a swollen mass of blood and bruising, she returns to the motel room with a pizza to find David has locked himself in the bathroom. Sitting on the bed, Katia resigns herself to wait. After a time, David bursts naked from the bathroom screaming inarticulately. His already distorted features are rendered truly monstrous, having cut off his hair, bald save for sparse patches here and there. Leaping on top of Katia he repeatedly stabs her with a pair of scissors, his frenzied, animal screams pulsing rhythmically as he drives the blade downwards. In these bursts of violence the strain of miscommunication gives way to complete abandon in the couple's primal regression. The banality of tautological exchange, empty sentiment and pointless bickering dissolves into an inarticulate chaos of screams, cries, croaks and groans.

After the murder, we cut to the film's final image – a static, high-angled, extreme wide shot looking down at David's naked corpse in the desert. In long take we watch the attending police officer pace the scene, arguing through his radio with a colleague before he all but disappears, walking into the distance (see Figure 4.2). The officer's language is replete with generic cliché, uttering phrases including: 'Guy looks like he's been through a meat grinder, man.'/'I don't want this to turn into a spectator show,'/and 'Get your ass off the phone, stop talking to your wife, and get me somebody out here now!' This rhetoric is almost laughable for its performative ineptitude, like the clichéd sentiment of David's earlier, 'I'm happy ... to be here ... with you.' It is, however, entirely fitting, in keeping with the film's rendering of language as both surface and ineffectual. Reinforcing our position as alienated observers, this shot illustrates a world that persists without David and Katia, a world still characterised by miscommunication and conflict.

Adjusting our perception to see the final violence as part of a greater pattern of repetitive animosity, it is in fact inevitable from the outset that something grievous should happen. Far from an incongruous rupture, or directorial

Figure 4.2: The earth abides – the final shot in *Twentynine Palms*.

misstep, the violence of the film's ending is the natural corollary of violence threatened throughout. The couple, and the world they inhabit, bristle with tension; a frustrated inability to communicate with one another sees any kind of affection turn to self-destructive rage. Further, Dumont's scope vision landscape seems ready to swallow them at any given moment, and the inimical locals form a gradually encroaching presence. The film itself has a feeling of pent-up energy that needs to be worked out in the frequent fights and ferocious fucking. Its repetitive patterning of driving, arguments and sex gives the sense of a cable ever tautening and then slackening, until in the film's final minutes it finally snaps. When the film's eruption into violence does occur, rather than this constituting a drastic break with the orientation established earlier, it is rather in keeping with the film's pattern of spasmodic outbursts of energy.

The repetitive patterns developed in *Twentynine Palms* give the film a structural affinity with negative conceptions of the everyday. Its patterning of repetition through language and action is without consequence – rather it is mundane, banal, redundant. This is not the repetition of De Sica's maid grinding coffee in *Umberto D* – a repetition with creative potential and the prospect of self-discovery as described by Andrew Klevan (2000: 46–9). David and Katia's monotonous pattern of arguments and reconciliations is both constrained and incapable of speaking to anything beyond itself. Nor is the world invested with the prospect of self-realisation. David and Katia do not shape the space they inhabit, nor does it shape them. The *mise-en-scène* remains indifferent to their presence. Where the characters in Haneke's *The Seventh Continent* and Bresson's *Money* always hold the promise of an interiority that might yield an underlying coherence – a coherence that we are denied access to – David and Katia are so cut off from the world and each other that they give the impression of being thrown into it meaninglessly. Despite the film's analogous structure, Breillat's vastly different treatment of the same elements in *Fat Girl* both produces a different conception of the everyday, and drastically alters our relation to the violence that irrupts out of it.

FAT GIRL

> I want to speak of certain events of language, of words in themselves rich in repercussions, or words misheard or misread that abruptly trigger a sort of vertigo at the instant in which one perceives that they are not what one had thought before. Such words often acted, in my childhood, as *keys*, either because surprising perspectives were opened through their very resonance or because, discovering one had always mutilated them, suddenly grasping them in their integrity somehow seemed a revelation,

like a veil suddenly torn open or some outburst of truth. (Michel Leiris, 'The Sacred in Everyday Life', 29)

Originally published in 1938, Michel Leiris' brief paper, 'The Sacred in Everyday Life', recounts childhood memories pertaining to certain objects, places and words that he connected with a sense of the sacred – akin to the hidden totality I have described in earlier accounts of the everyday. Leiris' description of language in this paper is as a creative force: he describes words invented by himself and his brothers during play. A potential source of the uncanny, misrecognised words, once corrected, gained new significance for Leiris, in one instance evoking a feeling of 'triumphant discovery' (1988: 30). In another he found the words 'took on a resonance that was especially disturbing' (ibid.: 30). I mention Leiris' paper here, as it goes some way to illuminating the way language works in Breillat's *Fat Girl*, which I will show also embodies these two functions – the creative and the uncanny as a means of accessing profundity within the everyday. The creative potential of language in Breillat's film is significantly contrasted to its negation in *Twentynine Palms*, and influences the film's orienting structure of proximity.

As in *Twentynine Palms*, much is made of language in *Fat Girl* as a key element. It is, however, far more vital and varied in Breillat's film. Rather than an unnatural abstraction which hinders understanding, language in *Fat Girl* is figured as having a creative potential. Ordinary words cast out of the mouths of the protagonists throughout the film seem both to shape the world they inhabit, and find their unhomely echo in the film's violent ending. In the opening scene, the sisters walk in the woods expounding their respective views on what it means to be a virgin. Anaïs explains her philosophy of sex: 'If I meet a man I love, I'd want to be broken in. He won't think my first time counts. The first time should be with nobody.' It is apparent that Anaïs is wiser than her years; tinged with a premature cynicism, her words are weighted with an adult grasp of the world (as though it was Breillat speaking rather than a child). Elena's, in contrast, are bound up in idealised romantic discourse. Anaïs wants to be 'broken in', whereas for Elena, virginity is 'what counts'. This disparity is emphasised again in a later scene when Elena asks for advice on whether or not to sleep with Fernando. Bewitched by Fernando's romantic gesture of an 'engagement ring', Elena tells her sister, 'I think I'm going to give myself to him tonight.' The language of sentiment is foreign to Anaïs, however, who responds bluntly, 'You use some really weird expressions.' Later in the conversation, Anaïs restates her position on virginity: 'Personally, I want my first time to be with a boy I don't love. Because afterwards you realise he doesn't love you or you don't love him, and you feel dumb.' Elena, speaking with the empty authority of her incipient romance, replies, 'You'll see when you fall in love.' But Anaïs remains stoic: 'I doubt it.'

These words about virginity, like many others in the film, are retrospectively understood to be imbued with a premonitory significance once considered in the context of the film's brutal ending: Elena's romantic ideals end in heartbreak as she realises she has been deceived, and Anaïs loses her virginity to a madman in a deeply ambiguous scene that begins as a rape, and ends as something less clear-cut. This motif use of portentous language, layered throughout but only recognisable as such at the film's end, possesses something akin to the vertiginous quality described by Leiris. The film's final events vest certain words uttered throughout with an ominous resonance that they do not possess at the time of their enunciation. It is not that we have misrecognised or misunderstood certain dialogue, but that it comes to carry significance beyond its immediate meaning, bringing us closer to the effective opening up of language in *Eyes Wide Shut*. Language in *Fat Girl* has a creative potential; in fact, we get the sense the girls' world is borne out of their words, as though conjured on their early woodland walk. While we cannot recognise the girls' discussion of virginity as foreshadowing at this early stage, Elena's challenge regarding who can pick up a boy first becomes immediately manifest, announced only moments before the sisters meet Fernando at a nearby café, and Elena's doomed romance begins.

Anaïs' relationship to the world and to language, which I have already described in terms of maturity, begins in this scene to be revealed as more than an affected adult rhetoric or a simple conduit for Breillat's ideology. Developed over the course of the film is the sense that Anaïs has a keenness of perception greater than that of any other character. As Fernando and Elena become acquainted – he is from Rome, she and Anaïs are on holiday but it is hard to leave their gated community – Anaïs looks on before interjecting, 'We're not allowed,' a comment which embarrasses Elena. 'Don't worry,' giggles Anaïs, 'he can't understand a word you're saying. He's just being polite.'

Immediately, Anaïs can read Fernando in a way that Elena and the girls' parents are blind to. In the scene immediately following the sisters' meeting him, Fernando is at the family villa for lunch. Despite the drastic age difference between Fernando and Elena (at least ten years), the girls' parents seem content with their friendship, even when Elena speaks of him in more familiar terms, stating that she will be putting him on a diet. When Mr Pignot asks where Fernando met his daughters (this is the only indication of wariness, being otherwise charmed by the man's aspirations to become a lawyer), his wife interjects before Fernando can respond. 'François!' she smiles embarrassedly. 'Young people meet. It just happens these days.' Mrs Pignot especially seems unable to interpret indicative nuances in behaviour of either daughter, constantly resorting to vapid maxims in lieu of genuine consideration: Anaïs eats so much because 'it's hormonal', she is upset because 'it's adolescence', and Elena has brought a man home because 'young people meet'.

In addition to its creative potential to shape the everyday, language also functions as a currency of power for those who understand its mechanism and can read others. In Anaïs, this is an admirable trait that helps elicit our sympathy; she warns her sister about Fernando's suspect gesture of a valuable engagement ring, and later consoles her in her heartbreak. However, in Fernando it is an opportunity for manipulation, as emphasised in his seduction of Elena. In their first night-time meeting, having snuck into the girls' shared bedroom, Fernando expresses frustration at the language barrier between them: 'I'm sorry I don't speak French very well. I'd like to tell you all kinds of things.' There is discussion about who will learn the other's language; Elena will take Italian at school next year, Fernando will learn French so that he might visit her in Paris. The irony here is that Fernando already speaks her language in the sense that he is able to exploit her quixotic rhetoric in order to procure sex. When denied vaginal intercourse, Fernando changes tack, insisting that consenting to anal sex would both allow her to retain her virginity and be 'proof of love'.

Elena's consent is hardly a clear endorsement; where she had interrupted Fernando's earlier attempts voicing her concerns, at this point she remains silent. Significantly, at the moment of penetration, Breillat cuts from a two-shot of the couple in bed to a close-up of Anaïs' face as she watches both curious and afraid. This reaction shot is held throughout; over Anaïs' nervous glances, we hear Elena's pained cries and Fernando's pleasured groans. This striking denial of visual access is not a substitution based on censorial grounds: the shot of the couple in bed is not explicit, and we have already seen a shot of Fernando's erect penis. Instead it continues another motif: that of watching Anaïs watching.

Indeed, Breillat devotes a significant amount of time to Anaïs' expressions, from the readily apparent to the illegible, as she bears witness to events around her. The later scene, in which Fernando has vaginal intercourse with Elena, likewise holds on Anaïs' response of silent devastation. Beyond developing sympathy for Anaïs, this attention to her expressions functions as a visual accompaniment to the keenness of her perception that we see in language and her ability to read others. Prior to Fernando's arrival, Elena has instructed her sister to go to sleep. 'You hear nothing, see nothing and know nothing.' Of course, Elena is demanding Anaïs be complicit in her forbidden tryst, but this line too gains resonance in our growing understanding that Anaïs' skill, or burden perhaps, is that she hears, sees and knows more than anyone else.

However, it is not just Fernando that Anaïs is attuned to. When the girls' father is called back to work, cutting his vacation short, Anaïs watches from the doorway as he packs his things. 'If he's flying back – ', Anaïs advances with concern. Mrs Pignot responds, explaining that she will drive, yet her daughter's apprehension is still not abated. Anaïs' foresight of course becomes significant in the fraught drive home during which a number of menacing trucks on the highway, coupled with her mother's growing fatigue and anxiety, imply a palpable threat to the family's safety.

Anaïs' attunement to the world around her helps bind us to her character; very rarely are we privy to a scene from which she is absent. She and Elena are the only characters that elicit sympathy; the girls' parents are patently self-absorbed, Fernando is selfish and manipulative, and his mother, whom we only see briefly, is theatrically exaggerated in her performance to the point of comedy. In contrast to Dumont's treatment of David and Katia as animals under observation, Breillat's film affords an involvement with Anaïs and Elena that suggests both depth and the potential for transformation. This involvement is intimately connected to a positive conception of the everyday, as a source of authenticity via the attention to nuance.

I want to turn now to an important moment that is best representative of what I am calling the film's proximate orientation. The moment is one of bonding between sisters and occurs across two consecutive scenes, shot in a succession of long takes. It is the evening that Elena will lose her virginity to Fernando, and the girls stand before the bathroom mirror (see Figure 4.3). In close-up, Elena puts her arm around Anaïs and leans into her, resting her head on her shoulder, and begins a monologue concerning how different they are. What we might initially anticipate to be more of Elena's vitriol – the pair have had a love/hate relationship throughout the film punctuated with moments of genuine cruelty – turns out to be an astute and sensitive reading of their connection. At first, Anaïs too seems uneasy in this embrace. 'No one would think we're sisters,' Elena begins, 'It's true. We don't take after anyone. It's like we're born of ourselves. It's funny. We really have nothing in common.

Figure 4.3: Sisterly bonding in *Fat Girl*.

Look at you.' As though in preparation for more insults about her weight, Anaïs shuffles, swallows, averts her gaze. Elena continues, 'You have small, hard eyes, while mine are hazy.' Anaïs adjusts her stance, as though to remove herself, but Elena grasps her anew, and continues: 'But when I look deep into your eyes, it makes me feel like I belong, as if they were my eyes.' At this, Anaïs' face lightens, revealing a subtle smile, and she responds, 'I feel the same thing.' Returning her sister's embrace, clasping Elena's hand in her own, Anaïs smiles, 'That's why we're sisters.' The pair concede that their hatred of each other is exacerbated by their difference, and negated by their likeness.

This conversation continues into the next scene, though it is clear some time has elapsed; the girls now lay side-by-side in Elena's bed dressed in their nightclothes. After more musing from Elena on their rivalry, the sisters reminisce stories of growing up together. Elena again teases Anaïs about her weight, but unlike her previous attacks, there is a gentleness here that neutralises her words, and a giggling Anaïs returns 'Bitch' in jest. Recounting her interpretation of their relationship as young children, Anaïs suggests that Elena's affection for her ceased the moment she grew to match her in size, strength and language. 'Really?' Elena replies. 'I don't remember that. Are you sure you aren't making it up?' Giggling, Anaïs mentions that in spite of their differences, most people do not bother to remember which sister is which, a point prompting Elena's laughter and agreement. The pair's stories soon deteriorate into bursts of infectious laughter, gripping them in involuntary waves, renewed time and again by each other.

These moments, surely the kindest in the film, strike me as central to what I am calling *Fat Girl*'s orientating structure of proximity, and are animated by the combined treatment of language and the insight we are provided into the characters' everyday outside of their present holiday setting. Where in *Twentynine Palms*, language is consistently the stuff of miscommunication and conflict, seemingly doomed to futile repetition, in Breillat's film it has creative potential. Like the film's motif vesting of language with the power to shape the world, Elena's words here are simultaneously of observation and creation. ('It's like we're born of ourselves'/'Are you sure you aren't making it up?'). Further, these moments also make real the unseen domestic elsewhere of home that has until now only been mentioned in passing. This sense of a shared history is again in drastic contrast to Dumont's hermetically sealed desert setting. We have heard about the girls' home on the outskirts of Paris in the conversations between Fernanado and Elena, and it is where their father must return early to deal with issues at work. While we never actually see this space, the sisters' bonding grants us a kind of imaginative access to a better world, albeit constructed, or reconstructed. It is not literally the space the girls' father has returned to; the space evoked here is something between imagination and memory – 'Are you sure you aren't making it up?'/'I remember it perfectly.'

Most importantly, however, these scenes show that the everyday, and one another, might be discovered through concentrated attention. Like Lefebvre's call to attend to the microstructures of the ordinary, Elena's attention to often ignored nuance allows a momentary acknowledgement and teasing out of strands of genuine human experience and connection amid the otherwise alienating space of sibling rivalry and self-absorbed parents. If Elena is unable to read Fernando, she seems here to have a genuine acuity for Anaïs. This is emphasised in contrast to her previous interpretations of Anaïs' behaviour, which often involved terse accusations of jealousy and attempts to replicate her. While there is probably truth in these claims, her snap dismissals are here replaced with a considered ability to articulate nuance. Elena's pause to offer a measured reflection on the sisters' differences and likeness is rewarded with these moments of genuine connection. These are the shades of distinction that are often overlooked; by Elena in her flippant labelling of Anaïs throughout the film, by the girls' mother in her innocuous platitudes, and by outsiders who do not care to distinguish between them.

The establishment of this warmth, however, brings with it the potential for its loss. While we expect this loss to come in the transition from child to adult – it is no coincidence that these scenes occur on the eve Elena will lose her virginity – we do not expect it on the level of the elsewhere crashing into the here and now. These moments of kindness draw us in, allowing the radical disorientation in the film's final minutes to be genuinely disturbing.

The arrival of Fernando's mother to reclaim her ring means the immediate termination of the family holiday, and the treacherous drive home begins. After Mrs Pignot breaks her silence to admonish Elena, Anaïs requests the car be stopped as she is feeling ill. In this scene, again, the girl's language takes on a conjuring quality, but like the other instances of this, it is only understood retroactively. Elena holds Anaïs as she vomits by the roadside, their mother leaning against the car in the distance, waiting. 'I hate her,' Elena cries, 'I wish she'd die.' We cut to a medium shot of mother, cigarette poised in one hand, the other propping up her elbow, disinterested. Elena continues, 'I don't care, I'll die with her.' Anaïs pauses, coughing, 'Speak for yourself', and spitting the last of the vomit from her mouth, 'I don't want to die.' Cars and trucks speed by in the distance. Elena counters, 'No danger of that. You're not in the dead man's seat.'[7] On the surface, these are the frustrated declarations of a teenager devastated by heartbreak, realising that life is unjust and parents can be unforgiving. However, in retrospect, these words inadvertently carry a terrible weight; by morning Elena and her mother will be dead, and Anaïs presumably would have succumbed to the same fate had she been seated in Elena's place. Again, words find their unhomely echo in the film's concluding violence, with a sensation akin to Leiris' sense of revelation in the wake of understanding previously mistaken aspects of language for what they really are.

The shock of violence, when it does arrive, is made all the more palpable by the fact that, despite Breillat's concerted efforts to invest the film's final sequences with an imminent sense of dread, we cannot see it coming. Where films like *The Seventh Continent* and *Money* pare back film style, levelling unexpected violence and the banal, *Fat Girl*'s final road sequences begin to freight the everyday with a menacing quality. In contrast to the desert of Dumont's *Twentynine Palms*, which is consistently indifferent to the couple and their squabbling, in the third act of Breillat's film we see a comparatively expressionist representation of the family's strain. Claustrophobic in the car, this building tension appears to spill over into the *mise-en-scène*. Much is made of the wavering position of the family vehicle consistently dwarfed on a highway otherwise populated by large trucks, horns blaring; David Bowie's 'The Pretty Things are Going to Hell' blasts through the radio, its volume jarring in an otherwise quiet film, and its ominous lyrics acquiring a sinister quality. In addition to the prospect of a car accident, Breillat points to other potential threats – having pulled over at the rest stop, Elena walks alone into the night to find a toilet, Anaïs locks eyes with the driver of a passing truck, and a point is made of locking the doors before Elena falls asleep.

While adding an ambient sense of threat to the world, these features contribute nothing to the potentiality or plausibility of violence as it does occur; rather they seem concerned with a more explicit misdirecting of our expectations. Furthermore, these cues significantly do not function like the generic signals we are granted in examples of contemporary French horror proper. The tension-building non-diegetic soundtrack that accompanies the lead-up to horror in films like *High Tension* (Aja 2003), *Them* (Moreau and Palut 2006) and *Frontier(s)* (Gens 2007) is absent; while Breillat does employ an eerie and sparse non-diegetic score, notably, this only begins after the violence has already commenced, rendering it a response rather than a warning. Where generic cues might at least signal us to expect disruption, allowing us to prepare somewhat, Breillat leaves us like Anaïs in the car, futilely locking the doors only to have a madman smash through the windshield.

The violence comes out of nowhere and is exacted with startling efficiency. The girls' mother is slumbering, and Anaïs has just consoled her forlorn sister with quiet words of wisdom and bid her lock her door and go to sleep. For a while we watch Anaïs sit awake in the back seat, chewing on a long rope of marshmallow. All is quiet save for some distant trucks and bird song. From Anaïs we cut to a reverse shot, her perspective looking at the windshield. Breillat affords us only a second to register the shape of a man's torso swinging a hatchet before the windshield is obliterated in a deluge of glass. Climbing onto the bonnet the stranger leans in and strikes Elena in the face with the axe, pausing afterwards to lock eyes with a terrified but silent Anaïs. The mother is only awoken as the man tears her dress, before strangling her to death.

That Anaïs' life is spared, in conjunction with the portentous use of language and expressionist *mise-en-scène*, has led some to interpret this violent event as taking place in the imagination of Anaïs. Indeed, one reviewer encourages such a reading in order to circumvent the horror, stating: 'The climax is distressing indeed, yet there is an interpretive escape route' (Groen 2001). Coulthard is more measured in her response, stating that the culminating violence in *Fat Girl* throws a range of interpretations into play: while we may interpret the ending as fantasy, it can 'also be seen as a diegetically real, brutal explosion of nonsensical violence that asserts the presence of the outer world on self-absorbed, contained bourgeois family life' (2010a: 66). Breillat herself neither confirms nor denies the suggestion of an imagined ending, preferring ambiguity, though it should be noted that despite charges of absurdity of the film's climax, it was inspired by a news article (Sobczynski 2004).

Like *Twentynine Palms*, *Fat Girl* too ends with the discovery of violence by the police. This time multiple officers form a crime scene, some bagging evidence while others escort Anaïs from the woods after her attack. Her final words, 'Don't believe me if you don't want to', are in response to one officer's comment to another about Anaïs' claim that she was not raped, and yet like other instances of language in the film, these words open up rather than enclose meaning. 'Don't believe me if you don't want to' is less an admittance to potential untruth (I may have lied to you, you may find that I was indeed raped), than it is a gesture towards an epistemological uncertainty in matters of consent (rape is a matter of conjecture, I 'know' I was not raped because I did not allow myself to be raped, but you may 'know' otherwise depending on the terms you bring to determine what 'rape' is). Those who take the final violence to be the product of Anaïs' imagination may also interpret her statement differently; J. Hoberman (2001) states that with these words, the possibility of the fantasy interpretation 'doubles back on itself'. Importantly, these words again point towards a use of language in which meaning is not fixed; language has the potential to shape the world, whether by Anaïs' creation of wholly imagined events or by her suggestion that the status of events is, like the shared history of the girls' bonding, not objective but susceptible to opinion.

I spoke earlier of the final shot of *Twentynine Palms*, in which the attending police officer argues with a colleague over his radio, as indicative of the persistence of a world fraught with both the superficial and conflicting. Where the world of *Twentynine Palms* endures without David and Katia, at the end of *Fat Girl* it literally stops as we hold on the freeze-frame of Anaïs' inscrutable gaze for approximately eighteen seconds before the credits roll (see Figure 4.4). Like her final enigmatic words, her face here opens up potential meaning rather than clearly defining it. Breillat once again implores us to study Anaïs' face, yet where her expressions had previously been clearly legible, here her countenance is sullenly defiant.

Figure 4.4: The earth stops – the freeze-frame that ends *Fat Girl*.

Regardless of whether we take the violence to be objective or subjective, the film's dénouement constitutes a drastic shift in its orientation, and its quality as disturbing is dependent upon our prior involvement. Through the insight given into the characters' shared history, the vesting of language with a world-making quality, and attention to and acknowledgement of that world, Breillat's film crafts a proximate orientating structure. The everyday crafted in *Fat Girl* is one open to possibility and one that rewards attention to nuance with genuine human connection and the potential for self-realisation, and yet with that acknowledgement of the world comes the potential for its loss.

Dumont's film, by contrast, depicts a world already closed off; David and Katia are stuck in alienating patterns of repetition which extend beyond the micro level of dialogue and action, to structure the film as a whole. If, in *Fat Girl*, language makes the world and has the potential to transform those within it, in *Twentynine Palms* it is more akin to the Old Testament's tower of Babel, already collapsing and alienating those in its wake. David and Katia cannot acknowledge one another, cannot reach a level of mutual understanding, because meaningful communication itself is impossible. The violence of *Twentynine Palms* is the culmination of latent enmity throughout the film, from the couple's frequent and frustrated implosions, to the hostility of those they encounter. And yet the world they inhabit is unresponsive to their presence and enduring in their absence. This is in stark opposition to *Fat Girl*, whose key characters seem to shape the world as they inhabit it, to the point where the *mise-en-scène* comes to absorb their strain, and to the point where the verity of events is beholden to their interpretation.

Despite the structural affinity of *Fat Girl* and *Twentynine Palms*, the affective quality of the violence that erupts in their final moments is different in the two films. Attempts to explain this violence in terms of sudden shifts in genre have been useful as far as they go, but they only go so far. Instead, examining these turns to violence not as isolated devices, but in the context of their nuanced relation to the everyday, we are afforded a better insight into how the films grant or withhold a means of understanding the violence they depict. The following chapter considers how disturbing cinema's preclusion of textual closure not only extends its affective quality, but makes a bid to unsettle the viewer's own conception of daily life with analyses of Gaspar Noé's *I Stand Alone* (1998) and Markus Schleinzer's *Michael* (2011).

NOTES

1. The nature of this event, as rape, or not rape, is highly contested. For reading on this issue see: Fox-Kayles (2010: 15–26); Horeck (2010: 195–209); Maddock and Krisjansen (2002: 161–71), Wheatley (2010: 27–41).
2. Generically speaking, Beugnet's employment of the term 'teen movie' feels inaccurate, for it seems to suggest the film not only depicts the teenage experience, but is aimed at teenagers. While Peter Sobczynski (2004) has noted the film's premise – a challenge between two adolescents to see who can lose their virginity first – 'sounds like the set-up for a romp not unlike "American Pie,"' the film shares more in common with coming-of-age dramas like *My Summer of Love* (Pawlikowski 2004) and *Fish Tank* (Arnold 2009).
3. For Thomas, broad divisions between the perceived malevolence and safety of any given film world can be charted onto the wider distinction between comedic and the melodramatic registers. Specifically, this distinction is between categories that fundamentally go beyond genre, rather than constituting genres themselves. These categories are both structures – each have their own tendencies to organise narrative space in particular ways – and 'ways of being a genre film', in the sense that *Blazing Saddles* (Brooks 1971) and *The Searchers* (Ford 1956) are both Westerns, operating in alternative registers (12). Significantly, Thomas argues, individual films often oscillate between the comedic and the melodramatic, while 'A film's generic identity, on the other hand, tends to be more stable: a Western generally remains a Western all the way through' (2000: 14).
4. *Twentynine Palms*' characters frequently shift between speaking French and English as they attempt to communicate with one another. Because I take these changes to be significant in illustrating the film's shaping of the everyday as alienating, I have opted in this case study to list both the original French and its translated English to transparently reflect where these changes come into play.
5. Thomas Demand is a German artist who works in a range of mediums. His video art, specifically, is often concerned with repetition and themes of latent violence in the banal. His 2001 work *Escalator*, for example, is a stop-motion animation looped recording of an escalator made out of paper. Aside from its repetition and ordinariness, it is also a recreation of actual surveillance footage from a London escalator in Charing Cross which was the scene of a murder. Similarly, Demand's 1999 piece *Tunnel* is both a looped shot of a driver's perspective driving through a white pillared tunnel (created from paper), but also a reference to the scene of Princess Diana's death (Heiser 2003).

6. This translates literally as 'Why are you thinking?' – an example of Katia's sometimes poor French. Her accent, too, oscillates between French and Russian, making her at times difficult to understand.
7. A colloquial French term for front passenger seat.

CHAPTER 5

Return to the Everyday

I Stand Alone/Seul Contre Tous (Noé 1998), *Michael* (Schleinzer 2011)

> In our ordinary experience of the world, nothing outside of us singles out for our attention the most significant aspects of, and patterns in, the space-time slices we perceive. Nothing presents us with the telling close-up or the synoptic long shot, and nothing cuts the moments of perception into a segmented, transparent ribbon that adheres to a 'dramatic logic' in the visible action. For this reason, the phenomena we witness often appear to us as puzzling, indeterminate, ambiguous, and without a guiding structure. This is a fundamental truism about our fragile perceptual connection to the world and, as a fact about our universal limitations as perceivers, it is one that has the deepest human consequences. (George M. Wilson, *Narration in Light*, 90)

After the mystery at the heart of George Sluizer's 1988 film *The Vanishing* has been resolved, and the film's protagonist has been murdered, that is, after the disruptions to the everyday, we see a return to it. In the film's final moments, the camera at ground level on a lawn focuses on a praying mantis clinging to a blade of grass, before tracking and tilting upwards to capture housewife Simone who waters plants with a watering can. She turns her head momentarily to glance at her children playing in the garden. We then see her husband Raymond in repose, his expressionless face propped up by his hand, mind seemingly elsewhere, a book abandoned by his side. This imagery of a relaxed weekend at home is set against the preceding scene in which the film's protagonist, Rex, awakens in the darkness of a makeshift coffin to realise that Raymond has buried him alive. The live burial is horrifying: we watch Rex alternate between futile screams and hysterical laughter as the flame of his cigarette lighter tapers out. But perhaps more troubling here is the juxtaposition of these shots with others depicting a family at rest. In part this pertains to the discrepancy between our awareness as to what Raymond has done, what lies under this earth, and his family's blissful ignorance. But bound up in this is the sense that, in spite of what we have just witnessed, this family will carry on as they always have, and that the rhythms of daily life will persist unabated.

It is this sense of the everyday as a force that endures, regardless of interruptions, that this chapter will consider. The representations of violence I have been charting are connected through their apparent disruption of the everyday: an everyday which, with the exception of *Salò* and *Come and See*, otherwise dominates the films' duration. Notably, more often than not, this disruptive violence occurs at the end of the films. Very rarely are we afforded a sense of the way in which the world will continue after these moments, though, of course, it will; in a paradoxical dynamic the violence both closes the film (the film ends) and leaves it open (we cannot contain its meaning). In contrast, this chapter examines films that draw attention to the persistence of the everyday, and the persistence of violence within it. Where many of the films cited earlier end abruptly after their violent disruptions, Gaspar Noé's *I Stand Alone* and Markus Schleinzer's *Michael* are significant for their contemplation of what a return to the everyday might look like. More troubling still is their implication that violence and the everyday are perhaps not mutually exclusive.

EVERYDAY TIME

To imagine an everyday that persists beyond the violent disruption, the 'lightning that illuminates the banal' (Lukács 1974: 153), is to acknowledge its peculiar relationship to time. For Lefebvre, the tension is between two modalities of time: the linear and the cyclic. On the one hand, everyday time is linear – an abstract but progressive chart made up of the things we do, the events that punctuate our days. This is the time of calendars, of narrative history, an imposition on the natural in order to account for it. In opposition is the persistence of circadian rhythms that Lefebvre calls cyclic time. Cyclic time pertains to a pastoral understanding of the world, the relationship between the human and the natural, which is in tension with modernity's imposition of linear time as a means to account for our existence. For those who subscribe to a positive conception of the everyday, it is in the uneventful that profundity is located if we only attend to its significance. Alternatively, in negative conceptions of the everyday, the cyclic is the space of alienation which must be transcended in order to access authentic experience. And yet, complicating matters is that the linear and cyclic are intertwined. Linear time is progressive, eventful, imposed; it subsumes the cyclic and yet it is necessarily bound up with it (Lefebvre 2008 v3: 11–12). Michael Sheringham calls the tension between these two modes the everyday's 'bewildering ambiguity of temporality'; it is 'both cumulative and non-cumulative' (2006: 33).

The distinction between cumulative and non-cumulative time presents a way of comprehending the world, and was crucial to the *Annales* school founded in France in 1929 which sought to reconceptualise the recording of history less as a linear record of events and individuals and concerned rather with the micro detail of the everyday, the *longue durée*. Frustrated with what he perceived to be the reductive oversimplification of traditional narrative history, Fernand Braudel, a key member of the *Annales* school, argued against the tendency to narrativise the grand scale of the world to render it legible. For Braudel, to define the world in terms of a linear narrative consisting only of the eventful is to impose abstract parameters divorced from reality. It was to falsely project 'a world, torn from its context'; problematically, such a vision would give the impression that history is 'nothing but a monotonous game, always the same ... governed by the eternal, pitiless recurrence of things' (Braudel 1980: 11).

Frank Kermode likewise describes the imposition of narrative structures onto lived experience as a means of satisfying a fundamental human need for meaning. Kermode considers the narrativisation of the world to be in accordance with apocalyptic thinking, which 'belongs to rectilinear rather than cyclical views of the world' (2000: 5). The Bible, for example, provides a renowned historical trajectory from beginning to end, starting with the creation of the earth and concluding with a projection of its annihilation. This linear structure, akin to that of basic literary plots, is unitary and concordant (ibid.: 6–7). Significantly, Kermode argues, it is a model that we adopt to make sense of our existence. Born *in media res*, humans project fictive origins and endings in order to make sense of the interim, and thus render it tolerable (ibid.: 7). The apocalyptic is demonstrated to be an endlessly renewable model of thought; undermined time and time again by the endurance of the world, the narrative is revised rather than discarded (ibid.: 8).

In a comparable vein, Lauren Berlant describes the condition of 'cruel optimism', noting the tendency for people to remain attached to an illusory concept of the 'good life' in the face of its deteriorating plausibility. Social equality, enduring relationships between couples and families, job security and the potential for upward mobility are among the several 'fantasies' that are upheld despite their status as increasingly precarious in modern, liberal-capitalist social structures. For Berlant, such fantasies are not just maintained as a means through which we get by day-to-day, but are also deeply attached to our sense of meaning; it is through these fantasies that people contrive an understanding of 'how they and the world "add up to something"' (Berlant 2011: 2).

The desire to place narrative parameters upon the world, in spite of its persistent undermining of these narratives, signals both a need to make the infinitely vast, graspable, and to construct an orienting sense of context in which the individual has purpose. Significantly for Berlant, it is not just our allegiance to a progressively tenuous narrative of the good life that is at odds with reality, but the contemporary discourse of trauma which conveys the historical present as a glitch in the ordinary fabric of things (Berlant 2011: 9–10). As Berlant argues, 'Crisis is not exceptional to history or consciousness but a process embedded in the ordinary that unfolds in stories about navigating what's overwhelming' (ibid.: 10). For Berlant, the everyday is in a deadlock to which crisis gives form, in response to which we adjust 'to newly proliferating pressures to scramble for modes of living on' (ibid.: 8). In this sense, crisis becomes ordinary, and what is truly significant is the means by which we appropriate catastrophe.

In Kermode's assessment, our adjustment to the events that undermine our imposed narrative shares an affinity with narrative fiction which employs sudden turns of events that require us to adjust our expectations (2000: 18). Such narrative twists, or 'peripeteia', both rely on our trust in the end, and bespeak our desire to reach it via novel and edifying means. Therefore our incorporation of these peripeteia in narrative fiction enacts the process of reframing belief in an end, as in apocalyptic thought. Significantly, however, Kermode links the disruptive event in narrative fiction to an expectation of revealed meaning and authenticity. Fictional works that incorporate peripeteia provide us with a means to play out 'the familiar dialogue between credulity and scepticism'. The more audacious the twists, Kermode argues, the more we are likely to feel that fictional work 'is finding something out for us, something *real*' (ibid.: 18).

Over the course of this book, I've spoken a great deal about the various ways examples of contemporary European art films deliberately hinder our attempts to interpret violent acts. Rather than offering a concordant beginning and end, and having us enact a process of readjustment of our expectations ultimately leading to understanding, these films, by thwarting our attempts to contain violence via various manifestations of what I call disturbing aesthetics, instead call into question the narratives and constructs we project. Where previous chapters have explored how this occurs in relation to stylistic and structural elements, this chapter will now turn to films that call our attention to the workings of time as a means of undermining closure. I argue that this dual conception of time as perpetual and cumulative is important to the way the films in this chapter extend their grip beyond their duration and how this dual conception informs the viewer's own understanding of the everyday they return to.

I STAND ALONE

Gaspar Noé's debut feature *I Stand Alone* is set in France in 1980, and follows an unemployed horsemeat butcher[1] who feels impotent in the machinations of a life he cannot control. The film forms something of a sequel to his 1991 short film *Carne*, which depicted the butcher's assault on an innocent construction worker whom he mistakenly believed had raped his mute teenage daughter. The events of *Carne* are condensed in *I Stand Alone* into a short montage, the remainder of the feature picking up where the short leaves off, showing the aftermath of this event on his life following his release from prison. Bidding his daughter goodbye in the psychiatric institution that has cared for her during his sentence, the butcher leaves Paris for Lille to move in with his emasculating mistress (now pregnant) and her mother. When accused of infidelity, the enraged butcher beats his mistress to abort the child, steals a gun and flees back to Paris. For the most part, we follow the butcher's unsuccessful attempts to find work and borrow money from old friends, as he grows increasingly frustrated. Down to his last francs and filled with rage at the constant rejection, the butcher resolves to use the three bullets he has to kill those who he feels have wronged him. Instead, however, he collects his daughter from the institution, bringing her back to the slipshod hotel in which she was conceived, and struggles to decide whether or not he should give way to his incestuous desire for her, and kill them both. We see this murder/suicide decision play out with graphic violence. However, it is later revealed to have taken place only in the butcher's imagination. Resolving to take the 'moral high ground', he puts his gun away and breaks into tears of love for his daughter. It is implied that he still has sex with her. However, the butcher's narration frames this in the context of true love and the film ends on a comparatively cheerful note as he contemplates his happiness in this moment and the possibilities of the future.

I Stand Alone is extraordinarily bleak, dominated by an oppressively pessimistic narration as the central character spits misanthropic vitriol throughout. It is also characterised by an aggressive style established in *Carne*; intertitles reminiscent of Godard's *Weekend* break up the narrative and give further weight to the butcher's mentality with statements such as JUSTICE, MORALITY and LIVING IS A SELFISH ACT. Rapid camera movements often accompanied by loud gunshot sounds or low note bursts on the soundtrack are also used to jolting effect. Notoriously, before the film's climactic act of graphic violence, namely the imagined murder of the butcher's daughter Cynthia, a title card warning the viewer that they have thirty seconds to leave the screening appears, which proceeds to count down before flashing with alarm sounds. These devices function both to draw us uncomfortably into the butcher's nihilistic subjectivity, while also self-consciously drawing on B-movie gimmicks.[2] If Haneke's *The Seventh Continent* and Bresson's *Money*, explored in Chapter 3, work to efface violence from the films' aesthetic, Noé's film is at the opposite end of the spectrum; violence has an ambient presence throughout, in the film's style and sound design even when not occurring onscreen, constituting a low-level continuous aesthetic assault.

While the film's aggressive aesthetic, with its startling sounds and abrupt camera movements, affects an immediate visceral response, I want to concentrate on another element that I think is crucial to the film's enduring unsettling quality, this being the treatment of time. *I Stand Alone* sees the butcher's move away from an alienated vision of the everyday to one of creative potential. This is simultaneously a move away from the determinism of an eventful, cumulative, narrativised conception of time, towards an embracement of the non-cumulative, slow moving, perpetual and indeterminate. As we will see, however, his discovery of the latent possibility to be found in an acknowledgement of the everyday is inextricably tied to his warped subjectivity, a fact that complicates this openness and draws attention to its implications.

Time is recurrently brought to our attention in *I Stand Alone*: from the butcher's incessant existential ruminations on life and death, his taking employment at a nursing home where he witnesses the passing of an old woman, intertitles that remind us of the time, date and location of events, to the film's climactic thirty-second warning countdown. I want to start, however, by considering the film's opening moments, which establish the determinist logic that will dominate the majority of the film, and which is significantly subverted by the film's end. This consists of a brief scene in a bar with characters whom we do not see again (something of a prologue to the film itself which thereafter focuses on the butcher), and a montage of images that introduce him as he narrates his life story from birth to the present.

The film opens with a bright red map of France, emblazoned with the letter 'F' as synthesised orchestral music plays. This is followed by a title card stating MORALITY, before a brief introductory scene plays out depicting a thirty-something year-old man speaking with bravado to some acquaintances in a bar about morality being the province of the rich. His posturing is underscored with sudden cuts to black and what will become a motif use of arresting bursts of sound. Another title card reading JUSTICE appears before returning to the man's gasconade. 'You wanna see my morality?' he asks, shortly before brandishing a handgun. 'Whether you're right, or whether you're wrong, same difference, friend.'

This scene establishes the film's tone. Immediately we enter a world in which the discrepancy in power relations between classes is acutely registered, and in which violence is understood to be the only means of levelling the playing field. The notion that autonomy for the downtrodden is only achievable through violence, a kind of flippant white man's bar-room appropriation of Franz Fanon, pervades the rest of the film, dominating the butcher's logic as expressed through his incessant voiceover and abhorrent actions. What we might otherwise be tempted to dismiss as the plight of one deranged individual is undermined by the film's prologue, which suggests on the contrary that this mentality is all-pervasive rather than isolated. The world we enter in *I Stand*

Alone is one of imminent danger; deadly force is established as the final arbiter of morality and, as will be conveyed throughout the film, 'morality' is a relative rather than objective term, beholden only to the whim of individuals.

This prologue is followed by rousing military music and a title card that defines the film as 'the tragedy of a jobless butcher struggling to survive in the bowels of his nation' before the film's title appears and the butcher's narration begins. 'To each his own life, to each his own Morality' are the butcher's opening words before he relates his life story in the third person up to the present day over a series of still photographs. Positioning himself as an everyman, the butcher describes his life as 'the story of a man like so many others, as common as can be'. That the story that follows could hardly be considered 'common' implicitly suggests that, in the world of the film, the ordinary is bound up in trauma. Abandoned by his mother at age two, and orphaned at age six when his father dies in a German prisoner of war camp, the butcher describes his sexual abuse by a religious instructor, before his life takes a turn for the better at age fourteen when, 'driven by survival', he learns his trade. Hard work and saving see him open a butcher shop at age thirty, a shop which, a few years later, becomes successful. He then fathers a daughter, Cynthia, after getting a young factory worker pregnant, but the mother abandons them both and he struggles on as a single father, his daughter mute. The onset of Cynthia's puberty gives stir to incestuous desire: 'She takes on shapes. The father, unwilling bachelor, must resist temptation.' Events take a turn for the worse again when Cynthia gets her first period. Not understanding what is happening to her body, she sets off to her father's shop but a worker attempts to seduce her en route. A neighbour delivers the girl to her father explaining what he has witnessed but, seeing blood on her skirt, the butcher instantly assumes she has been raped and runs off in search of the perpetrator, stabbing an innocent construction worker in the face. The butcher is sent to prison, Cynthia to an institution, and in order to compensate the surviving construction worker, he must sell his flat and shop. Upon his release some months later, the butcher takes a job in a bar and begins a relationship with the matron. The matron falls pregnant, sells her bar offering to buy a meat market with the money so they might start over in the north of France. Feeling he has no other options, the butcher bids goodbye to his daughter and moves into a cramped apartment with the matron and her mother. Despite feelings of alienation in his new surroundings, he resolves to forget his daughter and his past. Upon reaching the present moment, the butcher's narration shifts to the first person, simply concluding: 'There you have it, that's me. That's my life. But today I'm starting life over again. Yes, ladies and gentlemen ... Today, I'm resetting the counter.'

In the space of approximately two minutes, the significant personal events of forty-one years are condensed into a coherent narrative of cause and effect.

In this condensing is an effacement of the everyday as background, replete with contingencies; it is, rather, a straight trajectory punctuated and determined by the momentous. The butcher's narrativisation of his life plays like a synopsis of a Zola novel, in that his emphasis on his self-identification as a 'being of pure survival' with limited autonomy brings to mind a sense of naturalist determinism. The butcher's narration in this introductory sequence often renders him as a passive protagonist – many of the events described happen *to him*, rather than as a result of his actions. In the few instances where he does make choices (to have sex with the young factory worker, to stab an innocent man, to embark on a relationship with the bar matron), these are generally answered by a loss

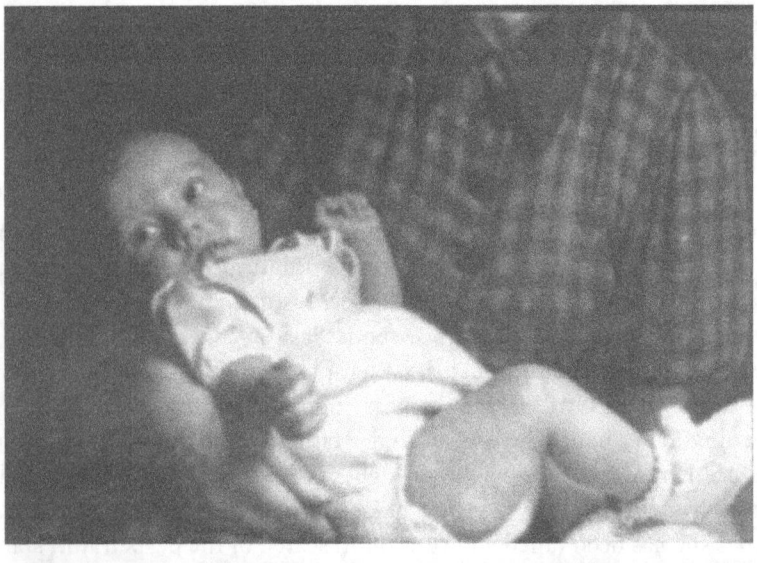

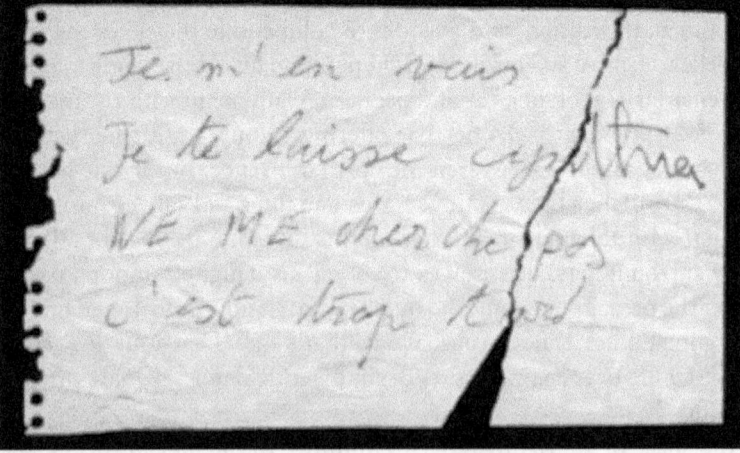

Figures 5.1–5.4: Narrativised time – excerpts from the opening montage in *I Stand Alone*.

of autonomy again – 'events precipitate', he is 'forced' to raise his daughter on his own, to sell his flat and his shop, and, 'having no other choice', agrees to leave Paris with the matron.

This determinist logic is emphasised with the montage of still photographs that underscore the butcher's narration. The plying of details to promote a scientific level of authenticity in the naturalist novel finds its cinematic echo in photos of the butcher from childhood to adulthood, snapshots of his shop and prison cell, along with crime scene exhibits and identification documents, serving to anchor his story with an evidentiary value (see Figures 5.1–5.4). Bleak and empty vistas locate us in Paris' industrial outskirts, which the

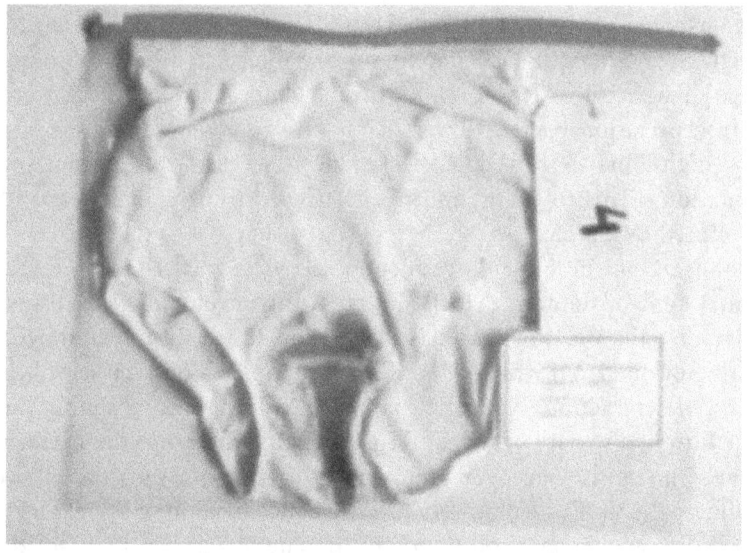

butcher's words populate with workers, neighbours, matrons – nameless icons of the working class.

Similarly, the title cards that appear throughout the film – announcements of the date, time and location of events, or block-lettered statements interrupting the film to accentuate the butcher's nihilistic mentality, seem to claim authority, and yet this authority is often undermined by what is presented. While not a direct representation of the butcher's voice (unlike his narration, they seem motivated by the film rather than its protagonist), these titles with their bold, forthright statements – DEATH OPENS NO DOOR or LIVING IS A SELFISH ACT, for example – seem to distil thematically the butcher's line of thinking. And yet, at other times, lone words onscreen – MORALITY or JUSTICE, for example – seem to function reflexively; unequivocal statements are interjected only to point to the absence of what they denote. The incongruence between these words and their interpretation by the film's characters – 'You wanna see my morality?' – highlights a troubling discrepancy between the absolutism their presentation seems to claim, and the relativism by which they are adopted and polluted onscreen.

Established in these two introductory scenes is what I take to be the fundamental logic of the film that the butcher must eventually turn away from, namely, that for the working class, everyday time is a linear trajectory of alienating events from which a level of autonomy can only be seized through decisive, violent action. Noé takes pains to reinforce this reasoning throughout the film in a variety of ways. Title cards that interrupt the narrative, the butcher's incessant voiceover and aspects of the *mise-en-scène* all work to promulgate the film's ideology – a morose concentration of social Darwinism in which life is characterised by a will to genetic survival in a world where everyone is alienated. Most prominently, this is conveyed through the butcher's narration, an oppressive and bleak series of observations that recurrently boil down to an animalistic essentialism. The world, according to the butcher's voiceover, is not civilised, but a jungle where only the strongest survive. The poor suffer at the hands of others, those with money can but cling to their façade of a loving family until the comforts of their material existence are stripped from them; as the butcher surmises: 'the day your life or house catches fire, when your middle-class dreams crumble, and you have no more to give, your brothers, your so-called friends will all join together to crush you'.

The butcher's narration is often characterised by a paring back of the positive aspects of human existence to reveal a fundamental ruthless drive of self-interest. Familial love and loyalty are theorised as schemes feigned only for the strategic betterment of one's own situation; sex passes the time, the butcher remarks, but is essentially 'nothing but a reproduction code written in your balls'. Similarly, the MORALITY and JUSTICE critiqued in the opening bar-room scene are concepts returned to throughout the film, figured as relative abstractions of an essentially primal drive.

Central to this logic is a distinction between autonomy and determinism, encapsulated by title cards late in the film that state: LIVING IS A SELFISH ACT. SURVIVING IS A GENETIC LAW. Over the course of the film we see the butcher's struggle to shift from one pole of this dichotomy to the other. We are constantly reminded of the butcher's desire to seize autonomy from what he perceives as an otherwise predetermined trajectory. Visiting a seedy porn theatre after witnessing the elderly woman's death at the rest home, the butcher philosophises:

Come into the world. Eat. Wag your bone. Give birth. And die. Life is a huge void. It always has been and always will be. A huge void which could manage perfectly well without me. I'm sick and tired of playing this game. No. No more. I want to live something personal, something intense. I won't be the last interchangeable cog in a huge machine. The day of my death I want to know that I've done more than the same crap done by a shitload of grovelling morons.

This logic of seizing autonomy through decisive action is also reinforced by the *mise-en-scène*. Early in the film, we see the butcher watching a cycling race on television. The commentator explains the qualities required to be the winner: 'He's got to know where to position his wheels when the going gets rough. He must know when to break away from the anonymity of the pack.' Reappropriated into the butcher's reasoning, however, this innocuous observation finds echo in the butcher's morally repugnant response to the world's determinism. Aborting his baby, abandoning his mistress and her mother, the butcher attempts to hitchhike, his voiceover asserting the integrity of this decision. He reasons that his child is 'better off dead', before resolving to do whatever is necessary to make it on his own in Paris. 'That's the only way to win. I've lost too much time as it is. And now, I've got a gun.'

The butcher's relocation to Paris to start over forms another false start in the search for autonomy. Time is again brought to the fore, as this transition fuels a sense of urgency; following the butcher's attempts to borrow money and secure employment, we are aware of his dwindling money and growing desperation, the gun increasingly featuring in his narration as a symbol of liberation. Down to his final francs, and feeling humiliated at the constant rejection, the butcher contemplates how best to dispense the three bullets in his possession, voicing increasingly sadistic fantasies.

It is in the film's climax, however, where the pivotal shift from determinism to autonomy takes place, and where the film's depiction of moral relativism is at its most troubling. The shift that occurs here overturns the film's driving logic – that violence is the only means to autonomy. This is simultaneously an overturning of the determination of narrativised time: the difference between the butcher's sense of powerlessness in his opening recount of his life story where 'events precipitate', and that seizing control of one's trajectory through violence (by forcing your overbearing mistress to abort as a means to escape a future you do not want, for example). Where we have until now seen only failed attempts at self-determination ('Today, I'm resetting the counter', 'I'm going to start my life over, all alone, in Paris'), this shift to autonomy can only genuinely occur with the butcher's turning away from violence as a means to self-realisation, and turning away from the narrativisation of determined time by forcing events. In its place, the butcher comes to embrace the indeterminacy of the everyday, the acknowledgement of time in the non-cumulative sense. This is to accept the world as boundless, in contrast to one's attempts to impose order and meaning upon it. As suggested earlier, however, with this openness and surrender of defined meaning come troubling implications.

Collecting his daughter from the psychiatric institution, on the premise that he wants to show her the Eiffel Tower, the butcher transports her instead back to the cheap hotel in which she was conceived. Interrupting their train journey is the motif jolting sound of a gunshot, and a title card reading: WARNING, followed by another, announcing: YOU HAVE 30 SECONDS TO LEAVE THE SCREENING OF THIS FILM. The seconds onscreen proceed to count down, over which the butcher's bleak narration continues. At four seconds, we get another title card reading: DANGER, which flashes alternately in red and black in time to an alarm sound, building a sense of urgency. Once the timer has clocked out, another jolting gunshot sound prompts a final title card informing us that the proceeding images take place at: HOTEL OF THE FUTURE 23RD OF MARCH 1980, AROUND NOON. After this, the pacing slows again as the butcher and his daughter enter the hotel room. There is a brief series of static shots as Cynthia looks around slowly as though in wait for further instruction. The butcher's voiceover relays his loosely connected stream of consciousness, before he finds his resolve to kill them both. Calm as they are, these moments are pregnant with tension. Staring at his daughter with his gun in hand, the butcher's voiceover gives his justification: 'Let's make this clear. The act of violence I must commit will be a wholesome act that will let us flee this machine with dignity.' What follows (we later find out) takes place entirely in the butcher's imagination, a scenario in which he molests his daughter, before suddenly turning to shoot her from behind, the bullet entering her throat. At this moment, the cinematography shifts from static shots to a shuddering handheld, rapidly reframing with zooms, and cuts which quickly alternate between the butcher, and his daughter dying on the floor. It is a horrific and viscerally affecting scene as we watch Cynthia shaking and gasping for breath, wide-eyed and still conscious, her throat pulsing blood.

The sense of urgency rapidly escalates here; someone outside bangs at the door demanding entry; cuts are again accompanied by jolts of sound; the butcher's narration grows faster, contemplating Cynthia's suffering and bidding her to die as he debates whether to put the girl out of her misery with a bullet to the head, or to save it for one of his enemies. Eventually he pulls the trigger, killing her instantly. This violence too happens onscreen in gruesome detail, and sets off an even more manic voiceover of disjointed thoughts, words colliding in overlapping monologue. Beneath this chaos of narration, the butcher starts humming, though this sound too is layered with anguished groans and the sounds of rolling thunder. With his gun pressed to his throat, the butcher begins a countdown from ten; each number introducing another disconnected idea, steeling himself for death before finally pulling the trigger.

Conveyed in this climactic scene of violence is the boiling over of pressure that has been latent throughout. The accelerated and increasingly disjointed thought process being narrated, collision of sounds, rapid reframing of an unstable camera, and fleeting inserts of bloody images (a replay of Cynthia's brains exploding, a baby being born, the butcher's imagined suicide) compete for our attention. Noé overloads us with sensory information, feverishly piling up images and sounds to involve us in the butcher's deteriorating sanity. The sense of urgency and stress affected in this scene is exemplary of the 'lapel grabbing kineticism' of Noé's style (Romney 2004) that first garnered the interest in him as a bastion of a new extreme cinema. What interests me here, however, is the relationship between this instance of abrupt and horrific violence and its greater context in a film otherwise lodged in the ordinary.

Arresting as these moments are, the disturbing quality of *I Stand Alone* is not limited to its instances of extremism; rather, I argue that it emerges in its relation between this violence and the persistence of the everyday in its wake. Following this cognitive assault, the film gains a renewed calm. Putting his gun away, and iterating his need to remain a good man, it is revealed that the preceding violence was subjective; instead the butcher clutches his daughter close and breaks into tears, Pachelbel's Canon in D Major welling melodramatically on the soundtrack. In a callback to the opening bar-room prologue, another title card – MORALITY – appears onscreen before an insert we have seen before (suggesting it is possibly still occurring solely in the butcher's imagination), a close-up of the butcher's hand unbuttoning Cynthia's jacket and pushing his hand between her thighs. MAN IS MORAL is the final title card that we see before the film's end, a sunset over a peaceful street as the butcher muses about the future.

In relation to the horrific violence we have just witnessed, the film ends on a comparatively happy note. Standing alone on the balcony, the butcher stares into the distance before Cynthia appears and wraps her arms around him. The butcher nuzzles her hand affectionately with his chin before turning to face her, bowing his head into the child's shoulder and rubbing her breasts. His narration resumes, though, for the first time in the film, it takes a positive tone. Where previously the butcher's voiceover had been characterised by its pessimistic determinism, the sense that everything was already tainted, here we see an openness to his rhetoric:

> I don't know how today's going to end. But here with you, I exist. And I'm happy. Happier than ever. The rest doesn't matter. Maybe it's our last day. Or maybe not. Maybe I'll never shoot myself. Maybe I'll make love to you. And tomorrow I'll be locked up. Four months, a year or two. So what? Jail isn't the end of the world.

At this point, the camera begins tracking leftwards, and cranes out to a quiet Parisian street at sunset. Birds fly in the distance. The butcher's musings continue, reasoning that at worst he can still commit suicide, but regardless of the outcome he will have this precious moment to remember, and the satisfaction of having acted autonomously. A group of children skip and run along the footpath into the distance, laughing gleefully. The butcher determines that he and his daughter's happiness should be their own province, rather than decided by the laws of strangers. 'In any event, whether we do it or not won't change the course of humanity. And for me, and for you, it'll change everything.' A little boy breaks away from the group below and runs towards us, crossing the quiet street and continuing out of frame (see Figure 5.5). The butcher's voiceover concludes: 'Between us, that's all I can see. I love you. That's all there is to it.' We linger several seconds more to contemplate this pastoral image, a child still visible at play in the distance before the credits begin.

What we see here is an aestheticisation of the everyday in coincidence with the butcher's acceptance of it. This concluding moment is both pleasurable and unsettling. After the sensory overload of violent images and jarring noises we have just been subjected to, it is hard not to be seduced by the beautiful image of a peaceful sunset on a quiet street. There is a palpable sense of relief as both camera and soundtrack have settled, and we are encouraged to absorb this moment, serene and picturesque. Likewise, the butcher's narration shifts from an alienated determinism to a de Certeau-esque embracement of creative potential and the autonomy of choice. The fundamental dichotomy between surviving and living that the butcher wrestles with throughout the film is reconciled here with a shift in language from the decrees of genetic essentialism to the musing of the possibility of individual happiness.

Figure 5.5: Aestheticisation of the everyday – the closing of *I Stand Alone*.

The aestheticisation of the everyday in this way calls on the tradition of its positive conceptualisation – that is, the school of thought that asks one to be present and attentive to the ordinary and overlooked in order to appreciate its totality. Such a rendering of the everyday, however, risks being stripped of its very ordinariness, as Sheringham observes by 'simply projecting onto the everyday values that are ultimately rooted in such non-everyday spheres as art, religion, or philosophy' (2006: 28). Henry David Thoreau's *Walden* is illustrative of this tendency in positive conceptions of the everyday when he connects 'the faint hum of a mosquito' to 'Homer's requiem; itself an Iliad and Odyssey in the air, singing its own wrath and wanderings.' Thoreau locates a profound artistry in that which is usually discarded. The mosquito's hum is not ordinary, but the locus of meaning, 'a standing advertisement, till forbidden, of the everlasting vigor and fertility of the world' (Thoreau 1965: 68).

By equating the buzz of an insect with ancient epic poetry, Thoreau appeals to the profundity to be discovered in the ordinary, if only we take the time to acknowledge it. Noé's concluding image to *I Stand Alone*, with its poetic rendering of the sun setting on children at play against a Parisian skyline scattered with birds, seems to operate in a similar way; the evocative strings of Pachelbel's canon in the scene just gone and the long take contemplation of an ordinary but simultaneously beautiful landscape seem to draw on the same vocabulary, and yet the nostalgic appeal of this image is in tension with the knowledge that this evocation of relief, beauty and the perpetuity of the everyday is occurring alongside a man's resolution to sexually abuse his daughter.

I mentioned earlier in this chapter that *I Stand Alone* could be seen as at the opposite end of the spectrum to the likes of *The Seventh Continent* in terms of its stylistic treatment of violence. Where Haneke renders the suicide of an entire family as banal an activity as making breakfast, Noé's style is hysterical and aggressive. The disturbing quality of Haneke's film is due in part to a refusal to stylistically acknowledge the weight of such a tragic event, indeed to strip it of its eventfulness. Alternatively, Noé's film, for a moment, seems to offer us a clear distinction between the dramatic and the ordinary in the revelation that the violence was imagined, and in the distinct transition between a nihilistic framing of the world to an embracement of its beauty and openness. What *I Stand Alone* shows in the persistence of the everyday after the surrender of a determinist framing, however, is not a positive and creative everyday free of the constraints of an abstract and imposed narrative order, but an indeterminate everyday in which the abhorrence of child abuse can comfortably exist within the banal; MAN IS MORAL, but morality is relative, itself an abstract imposition, unanchored to a shared understanding of the world.

In showing us a world in which a man can sexually abuse his mute daughter in the same space as we watch gleeful and unaware children play below, Noé's conclusion operates less as a juxtaposition of opposites than as a suggestion that human abhorrence and innocence are all cut from the same fabric. I want to suggest that the vision we are given at the end of *I Stand Alone* evokes the imagery of a positive conception of the everyday, in order to undermine it as naïve. The everyday that persists at the film's conclusion is not Thoreau's revelation at the beauty and pleasure to be garnered by acknowledging the everyday. It is rather an unsettling and seemingly contradictory blend of beauty and latent violence, an everyday which is not beholden to the narrativisation we attempt to impose in order to reconcile it to a clear and tangible meaning.

This idea that the beautiful and the abhorrent are intermingled within the quotidian is more closely aligned with the everyday evoked towards the ending of Vladimir Nabokov's *Lolita* than the exaltations of Thoreau's *Walden*. In contrast to Thoreau's lofty sentiments, the following passage from *Lolita* is powerfully evocative of the kind of everyday Noé represents at the film's end – a complex image where the richness and charm of the everyday is underscored by the base and repugnant. In this passage, the protagonist Humbert recalls a time many years past, just after the adolescent girl he has coveted has escaped.

One day, soon after her disappearance, an attack of abominable nausea forced me to pull up on the ghost of an old mountain road that now accompanied, now traversed a brand new highway, with its population of asters bathing in the detached warmth of a pale-blue afternoon in late summer. After coughing myself inside out, I rested a while on a boulder, and then, thinking the sweet air might do me good, walked a little way toward a low stone parapet on the precipice side of the highway. As I approached the friendly abyss, I grew aware of a melodious unity of sounds rising like vapor from a small mining town that lay at my feet, in a fold in the valley. One could make out the geometry of the streets between blocks of red and grey roofs, and green puffs of trees, and a serpentine stream, and the rich, ore-like glitter of the city dump, and beyond the town, roads crisscrossing the crazy quilt of dark and pale fields, and behind it all, great timbered mountains. But even brighter than those quietly rejoicing colors – for there are colours and shades that seem to enjoy themselves in good company – both brighter and dreamier to the ear than they were to the eye, was that vapoury vibration of accumulated sounds that never ceased for a moment, as it rose to the lip of granite where I stood wiping my foul mouth. And soon I realized that all these sounds were of one nature, that no other sounds but these came from the streets of the transparent town, with the women at home and the men away. Reader! What I heard was but the melody of children at play, nothing but that, and so limpid was the air that within this vapor of blended voices, majestic and minute, remote and magically near, frank and divinely enigmatic – one could hear now and then, as if released, an almost articulate spurt of vivid laughter, or the crack of a bat, or the clatter of a toy wagon, but it was all really too far for the eye to distinguish any movement in the lightly etched streets. I stood listening to that musical vibration from my lofty slope, to those flashes of separate cries with a kind of demure murmur for background, and then I knew that the hopelessly poignant thing was not Lolita's absence from my side, but the absence of her voice from that concord. (Nabokov 1980: 305–6)

Functioning in the same aesthetic vein as Noé's conclusion to *I Stand Alone*, Nabokov's style here imbues the details of the everyday with an enchantment born of their familiarity, reminiscent of positive conceptions of the everyday. Even so, the allure of this depiction cannot help but be haunted by the presence of its paedophile narrator, who is simultaneously separate from the world we occupy – it is from his distant vantage point that he observes the mechanisms of the world around him, but indeed the very conduit for our access to it. The picturesque and nostalgic scene that Humbert conjures for us is contaminated – most noticeably through the description of his nausea, but more insidiously by his subjectivity which imbues the familiar with the sexual as grasshoppers and the laughter of children 'spurt' from the landscape.

The problem Noé raises for us at *I Stand Alone*'s conclusion is in calling us to question the everyday we are left with at the film's close, in comparison to the everyday we entered at the film's beginning, and the significance of the transition. The film's closing long take invites our contemplation; Noé gives us the contrast between the calls of children at play in the street (gesturing towards a world that goes on), and Cynthia who is literally without a voice and whose future, indeed if she can have one at all, is at the hands of her father who had planned to murder her only moments earlier. It is a mixture of the simultaneously familiar and uncertain, the beauty of its openness and the terrible knowledge of what this openness means. Is this vision of an open everyday actually any better than the bleak but ordered world we were presented with at the start with its clear trajectory, Darwinian vocabulary and potential for closure? The butcher's understanding has taken a fundamental turn, and yet one wonders if this makes any difference in a world where concepts like morality are still unanchored to any shared meaning. Noé calls our attention to an everyday closer to that outside of the cinema: one that is open, indeterminate, circadian and not beholden to the narratives we impose to master it.

By representing the everyday in this way, *I Stand Alone* challenges the narrative we bring that violence and dramatic moments are isolatable and knowable, the lightning as opposed to the banal. Instead it depicts the everyday to be indeterminate – a complex and open mixture of high and low, indifferent to the narratives we impose because cyclic time is perpetual. Where *I Stand Alone* stylistically marks a clear shift from a linear conception of everyday time to a cyclic conception, and its undermining of narrative comes in showing this transition, Markus Schleinzer's *Michael*, by contrast, reveals the everyday to be a mixture of banality and horror within its first few minutes. Instead of a shift, the progression of *Michael* deepens our understanding of just how entwined these seeming opposites are. However, what Schleinzer's film also shares with *I Stand Alone* is the reassertion of cyclical time after the eventful and violent disruption as a means to destabilise the organising narratives we impose on the world and to foreclose our attempts to make sense of it.

MICHAEL

Michael opens with an evening in the life of its protagonist – a thirty-something year-old man pulls his car into the garage, and shuffles his groceries inside. He fries ham in the kitchen while the television news plays in the background. A view from the house's exterior shows electronically operated roller shutters slowly descending for the evening. Back inside, we watch as Michael fastidiously lays the dining room table for two. In the next shot, he unlocks and pulls open a heavy blue door, which opens onto darkness. We wait a moment staring in silence at the open doorway before Michael can be heard offscreen: 'Come on.' Again we wait; close to ten seconds pass before a small boy of about ten (listed in the credits as Wolfgang) slowly steps into the light. Frustrated, Michael pulls Wolfgang out, and prompts him upstairs. Over dinner, the boy asks permission to watch television, and after the pair wash their plates together, they do. Illuminated by the screen, Michael consults his watch before rising: 'That's enough.' Wolfgang tries to bargain for more time, but this is denied and he slowly stands, eyes fixed to the television trying to absorb as much as possible before he is sent back to the locked room. The remainder of the evening is depicted in fragments – upstairs, Michael reclines watching television, snacks from the fridge, has a cigarette outside, and brushes his teeth, before heading downstairs with a bottle of lubricant, closing the big blue door behind him. The camera remains fixed on the door for a few seconds before a cut to Michael washing his penis in the bathroom sink tacitly confirms what we already know. In the next shot, Michael marks the occasion in a day planner with a small symbol, replacing the book in a drawer before Schleinzer cuts to the opening title.

Established in this opening sequence is the film's relationship to everyday time, privileging the micro detail of the everyday with a kind of attention, seen in *Jeanne Dielman*, to that which usually forms the background for the eventful in films. Focusing on the relationship between the kidnapped child and his abusive captor, much of *Michael*'s ninety-six minute running time is spent tracing the banal day-to-day. Dramatic events are either elided completely – as with the sexual abuse in the opening sequence – or represented with the kind of stylistic flattening observed in Haneke and Bresson's films in Chapter 3. The repetition of actions and settings creates a sense of perpetuity: Michael's car entering and leaving the garage; the slow descent of the garage's roller door and the house's window shutters; shared meals at the dining room table; washing up; Michael watching television; smoking cigarettes; preparing for bed before the bathroom mirror; the opening and shutting of the blue door to Wolfgang's room; Wolfgang drawing pictures or playing alone are all recurrent images, calling attention to the way the horror of the eventful is realised within the ordinary.

Stylistically, the film is greatly indebted to the work of Haneke, for whom Schleinzer worked as a casting director on several films, and whom is thanked in *Michael*'s closing credits. Schleinzer adopts Haneke's sparing and distanced aesthetic; the film's attention to the banal, fragmented and observational style, cool colour palette, reluctance to provide access to character interiority, and reliance on diegetic sound, render a depiction of daily life that has much in common with *The Seventh Continent*. Like Haneke and Bresson's stylistic levelling of the eventful with the everyday as explored in Chapter 3, *Michael*'s flattening of child sexual abuse into the progression of mundane domestic routine (literally so in the opening sequence, with the registering of it in a diary under an earlier entry: 'TV') deflates the sense of drama such an act of sexual violence seems to demand. Rather than occupying a separate dramatic space, the abuse is represented through its equation with the ordinary. Not only does the transition from the closed door to a shot of Michael washing his genitals confirm what has occurred offscreen, there is an added cruelty in its curtness; what should be an appalling and dramatic event (even if it is not shown) is profaned further by its equation with the banal in the simple pragmatism of hygiene. Such a transition works to make violence present through its absence, and in turn the very ordinariness of washing oneself is contaminated. Like Bresson's displacement of violence onto everyday objects in *Money*, *Michael* plays the revelation of violence through the everyday as a kind of recurring manoeuvre throughout its duration. However, where Schleinzer's film differs is in the varied manifestations of this device and how it comes to deepen our perception of the latent violence in the everyday as the film continues.

In addition to the Bressonian elision of the dramatic, we see violence expressed through the everyday in the sheer ease with which the two seemingly opposite poles coexist, and even complement one another. Primarily this is evidenced in Michael's personality and engagement with others. Though not encouraged as a source of identification, Michael is hardly represented as a monster. Unassuming and private, Michael manages to keep up appearances with his family and colleagues with what appears to be the bare minimum of interaction – exchanging gifts with his sister at Christmas, reticent small talk at his work as an insurance salesman, and a ski trip with male friends. Ironically, this same circumspect temperament that helps to conceal his crime makes him the ideal candidate for a promotion at work.

As a pair, Michael and Wolfgang's interactions are so habitual – they eat meals together, clean, watch television, play, do jigsaw puzzles, and so on – that in many ways their relationship resembles that of father and son. This is emphasised on an outing to a zoo, when Michael and Wolfgang blend inconspicuously with other families. Beyond calling attention to the congruence of the ordinary with the abusive, this sequence takes a step further to highlight our need for these poles to remain separate, and our discomfort in their ambiguity. On a walking trail Michael and Wolfgang cross another man and boy, Wolfgang turning his head curiously after they have passed by. The uncertainty sparked in this moment, the suspicion that they too might not be what they seem, is one that thwarts an attempt to isolate Michael and Wolfgang's bond as other; instead, this move, like the bar-room prologue in *I Stand Alone*, implies the potential for violence in the everyday as ubiquitous.

The film is characterised by this entwining of the violent and the everyday, not as a recurrent move that steadily divorces violence from meaning, but as one that works to deepen our understanding of its interconnectedness.

Another example of this comes in a sequence that gradually reveals the intention for violence through ordinary objects. Walking through the children's bedroom section at a furniture store, Michael pauses momentarily to inspect a bright red racing car-shaped bed emblazoned with flames before moving on. We cut to Michael and Wolfgang assembling a bunk bed in the latter's bedroom. 'There's a piece missing', Wolfgang points out. Michael holds the frame while Wolfgang searches for it. In the next shot, Wolfgang is alone, his little hands making decorations – a childish multicoloured bunting out of crepe paper and string, which he proceeds to fix to the bed frame with sticky tape. Sitting on a play mat by the bed's base, Wolfgang concentrates, sorting children's books into two piles. One pile is carried to the top bunk and placed on a folded blanket.

If we have not already attuned to the significance of these objects, the following scene lays bare their purpose. From the quiet of Wolfgang's bedroom, we cut to the roar of speeding go-carts at an indoor track. Michael wanders the perimeter, stopping now and then to converse with young boys watching the race. Finally, a cut takes us outdoors, as Michael crosses the car park, a small boy in tow, the two engaged in a conversation about radio-controlled cars. 'Mine's all red. With sort of flames on the side … Maybe we can race sometime?' Michael says. We watch them stroll a fair way from the venue before an offscreen voice – the boy's father – beckons him back, reprimanding him for wandering off. Michael continues walking at a steady pace, head bowed, making a casual escape. Back in Wolfgang's room, Michael must deliver the news: 'The telephone rang just as I got in and they said the other boy couldn't come today. It's a shame. After we tidied everything up so nicely.' A reverse shot shows Wolfgang, sitting on the lower bunk, head bowed in a frown of disappointment. 'Don't be sad, OK?' Wolfgang shuffles slightly, his lower lip alternately pursing and relaxing as though to keep from crying.

There is, of course, the gradual revulsion at realising Michael's true intentions in shopping for and then constructing a new bed in Wolfgang's room. The red racing car bed that we see in the furniture store – what we might reasonably assume could be a present for Wolfgang – is instead revealed to have been recruited into Michael's imagination to an even more troubling end: a very nearly effective lure of another victim. And yet, as with the pair's encounter with strangers on the nature trail, Schleinzer's entanglement of violence and the everyday unsettles attempts at containment and clarity. That is, the film presents the everyday as already, and always, contaminated by violence and its potential. So entwined are these two things that the dramatic locus of the scene is divided between the threat of further abuse, and the day-to-day scenario of having to manage a young child's disappointment.

So far, I have been discussing the recurring move of Schleinzer's film to reveal violence as intrinsic to the ordinary in a variety of ways. What really extends our understanding of this dynamic, however, is the film's treatment of everyday time as circadian, in subtle but deeply troubling ways. It seems we are following the characters for a few consecutive months; about a third of the way through the film, we watch Michael and Wolfgang spend Christmas together, and towards the film's end Michael is killed, an event that the priest conducting his funeral announces to have occurred on the 26th of February. In contrast to *I Stand Alone*, however, *Michael* is far less explicit in providing us with a gauge by which to measure narrative duration. This lack of clarity is itself significant to the film's impact, for subtle indications of the perpetuity of Michael and Wolfgang's time together are themselves instances of the film's signature move that filters violence through the everyday. Like the abrupt cut that casually elides the abuse in the opening sequence, these moments are acerbic in their lack of emphasis. In one instance, Wolfgang watches silently as Michael hammers a cut Christmas tree into its base. Turning from his work to meet Wolfgang's sullen gaze, Michael's words are simple and cutting for their revelation that this is most likely not their first Christmas together: 'Why don't you fetch the decorations for once? The boxes are in the hallway.'

Perhaps the most potent example, however, occurs early in the film when we start to get a sense of Wolfgang's routine. One gathers that, for the most part, the boy is left to his own devices in his bedroom, an always locked but large, self-sufficient space complete with bed, toilet, sink, toys and food stores. A fragmented look at how Wolfgang spends his time when not in Michael's company sees him reading, waiting for the kettle to boil in preparing an instant meal, playing with toys, drawing, and writing a letter to his parents. Presumably the following day, we watch Wolfgang wrapped in a towel, holding the envelope containing his letter and drawing, while Michael carefully trims the boy's hair. In the following shot Michael sits alone, examining the envelope's contents. A cut transports us to the basement, Michael placing the envelope in a box full of undelivered letters – at least fifty – before restoring the box to its concealed home on the shelf (see Figure 5.6).

Again there is a callous weight to the nonchalance of these moments which call attention to the indifference of circadian time, this indifference being key to the films in this chapter's disturbing aesthetics in their calling attention to the fallacy of projected narratives. In a sense, *Michael* internalises this dynamic through Wolfgang's letters – the narrative evidently constructed for him by Michael who has told him they are being passed on, and a narrative that, via his own form of 'cruel optimism', Wolfgang believes, or convinces himself to believe despite doubts to the contrary. This is revealed in a scene where, over dinner, Wolfgang recounts a news story he saw on television about the financial crisis and suggests that Michael may lose his job. Michael's typically blank composure shifts to simmering rage and in an act of abject cruelty he retaliates by retrieving one of the boy's past letters, hitting him in the face with it. 'Do

Figure 5.6: A history of abuse filtered through the banal – the casual reveal of Wolfgang's many letters in *Michael*.

you know what this is? It's your letter. Your parents don't even want to read it. And they don't want you to write any more. They've given away all your stuff and rented out your room. They're not interested in you anymore.' He shoves the letter into Wolfgang's face repeatedly during this rant, before dropping the open envelope onto the boy's plate and returning to his seat. 'And they said you should behave and do as I say,' Michael concludes. Removing the letter from his plate, the boy stares downwards with brow furrowed to keep from crying. For a silent moment he fidgets with the piece of bread on his plate, before emitting in a tiny voice, soft with pity, 'That's all made up anyway.' The delivery of these words, perhaps the act of enunciating something he has long suspected, seem to revitalise his anguish and his facial muscles show great effort to refrain from bursting into tears. This scene is heartbreaking not only for its cruelty in watching a child's realisation or acceptance, whatever it may be, play out on a face that strains not to betray his loss of composure, but because immediately after we cut to the pair in the kitchen where life goes on. Wolfgang, seemingly reconciled for now, discards his letter in the bin before continuing to assist with the evening's cleaning routine.

Implied by the compatibility of violence and the everyday in *Michael* is that the separation of public and private spheres, the rituals of the everyday, and the systems we erect to maintain order and ward off chaos, have the dual function of perpetuating that which we seek to avoid. We might think of the institutions and rituals we construct as a means to 'ontological security' (Silverstone 1994: 19), and yet Schleinzer's film deals in the suggestion that these constructs are as much a potential incubator for violence as an inoculation against it. On the one hand we get a kind of inversion of the everyday; Michael's limiting of his involvement with others to conceal his crime is threatened by the humanity of those around him – on more than one occasion he rejects offers for the company of family members, and is almost discovered when a colleague who repeatedly tries to befriend him drops by his home unexpectedly. And yet, this is not to suggest that the film portrays the everyday as negative; it is not a matter of drawing a dichotomy between the alienating aspects of daily life, and the absence of an open attendance to its beauty. Michael and Wolfgang's everyday is unsettling and off-kilter precisely because it is so functional. The repetitions of the everyday that a negative conception would posit as the source of alienation, in *Michael* serve a dual function. The same constructs that allow for the abuse to continue (by insulating the domestic sphere from outsiders and maintaining a façade of normality) are integral to giving Wolfgang a sense of structure and continuity.

Michael entwines the banal and the violent throughout, showing them to be inseparable. However, I argue that the power of this move, its grip on us, is affected by the attention called to everyday time as circadian and indifferent. While the film displays various moments of disruption which seem to threaten the integrity of the pair's dynamic – Wolfgang falls gravely ill, Michael is unexpectedly hit by a car while crossing a busy street, and later is in danger of being stranded in the snow on a skiing trip – none of these events proves to be of great consequence. Rather they serve as minor interruptions, soon absorbed by the endurance of the ordinary. I want to turn now to the film's conclusion, as, in keeping with the majority of films explored in this book, *Michael* features a violent disruption to the everyday towards its end.

Feeling upbeat after his promotion party in the office, Michael returns home. Wolfgang is acting up, roaring and stomping about his room, jumping and swaying with excess energy, poking and clawing playfully at Michael who reacts with frustrated confusion. Michael delivers a left-over piece of cake, telling the boy not to eat it all before dinner, before going upstairs to have a cigarette, and prepare the table. In the meantime we watch Wolfgang fill the kettle with water and place it to boil. Because we have spent so much of the film watching its characters fill time, nothing seems amiss here. However, its significance is revealed when Michael opens the door to summon Wolfgang to dinner, the latter casting a jug full of boiling water into Michael's face. Wolfgang, seemingly shocked by himself, hesitates for a moment before making a run for the door, only to be blocked and, after a scuffle, thrown back into the bedroom where Michael manages to lock the child inside. Shivering with pain and almost blind, Michael showers himself with cold water before frantically struggling to place his key into the car's ignition. Traversing a dark and empty road, the car collides with a fence, flipping over an embankment and landing upside down, its headlights dimming to nothing. We are given

Figure 5.7: The routine replaces the dramatic in *Michael*.

a few seconds to process this, the shot remaining on the darkness, with only a few tiny lights flickering on the horizon to maintain a sense of space. In the next shot a recovery mission is already well under way, a fixed wide shot illuminated by the lights of various emergency vehicles (see Figure 5.7). Any shock of discovery or sense of urgency has been elided. Instead we are privy to a long take tableau of men at work, enacting the routine process of clearing a crash scene. To the right of frame, a pair of emergency workers load a sealed metal casket into the back of a van, while members of the fire department attach the wreckage to a truck-mounted crane. At the other edge of the frame, two police officers converse with a firefighter, though we cannot hear their words for the roar of idling trucks and the hauling machinery. Noticing the van removing the corpse has left the scene, one of the policemen extinguishes his cigarette to direct traffic.

The event of most consequence – the sudden death of the film's protagonist – is but a fleeting moment, already being cleared away. Its dramatic value is quickly deflected by its replacement with the obligatory processes it instigates. Structurally, the film enacts the ambiguity of everyday time as simultaneously eventful and non-cumulative, progressive and perennial.

Calling our attention to the endurance of the everyday, the film's final scenes follow Michael's family as they enact the necessary rituals and routines following sudden death. From the clearing of the accident site, we cut to an image of Michael's mother, sitting at a table littered with folded funeral invitations. Her red-rimmed eyes glisten, betraying recently shed tears, and with head bowed she sits almost perfectly still, completely absorbed in her grief. We watch her for a long time before the sound of the telephone jars the silence, stirring her back into motion. There is a slight shaking of her head, as though she is reorienting herself having been somewhere far away, as one who has been awoken prematurely from a bad dream. This is not the last time we will see her attention drift involuntarily. Later, while scrubbing the kitchen sink in her son's home, the gradual shift of her attention is legible as her motion slows to a standstill, her hand dropping as though acknowledging defeat. Her head droops and there is a pause while her face displays resignation to silent sadness; this is interrupted though when she raises a hand to wipe her nose. These scenes of banal but necessary tasks that follow Michael's death – funeral arrangements, cleaning, emptying the overflowing mail box, sorting through clothes – are perhaps the hardest to watch. It is not just that our attention is called to the persistence of the everyday, but we are made to attend to the weight of this persistence on the characters that remain. There is a palpable disparity between the gravity of this event on this family, and the pitiless endurance of the world around them. Like the cruel simplicity of Michael's collection of Wolfgang's letters, the indifference of circadian time is encapsulated in an image of Michael's mother and brother-in-law struggling with the accumulation of junk mail – that impersonal and disposable detritus of consumer culture – filling the letter box and jammed around the gate handle outside Michael's house. That these moments vest cyclical time with a sense of cruelty attests to the expectations we place in the narratives we impose upon our own everyday, outside the cinema.

Drawing on Kermode's argument about the narrativisation of experience, the means by which we assimilate disruption and the unexpected into our sense of the world and understanding of our place within it, my discussion of the films in this chapter has focused on how they both draw our attention to the dual structure of everyday time as simultaneously linear and cyclical, and the way this is used to point out the fallacy of these narratives we impose. Schleinzer's film makes explicit this human quest to impose meaning, and the folly of that attempt, in a scene towards its end, which depicts Michael's funeral. 'What should … what can … his death mean to us?' asks the young priest conducting the ceremony. 'Doesn't an early death – whether caused by illness or by a road accident – seem almost contrary to the ways of life?' After a pause: 'I say no.' The priest justifies this position by drawing on an anecdote about Michael's childhood impatience, suggesting that perhaps God grew impatient with Michael, thus beckoning him sooner than expected. In pat comfort to the aggrieved who are yet to discover Michael's crime, the priest manages in a brief sermon to all too neatly tie up the meaning of Michael's death, relating the unexpected horror of a violent auto accident to a benign episode from Michael's boyhood. Schleinzer highlights the feebleness of this ritual with an abrupt cut mid-sentence during the priest's conclusion: 'Saying farewell to Michael means –'

The weight of the inexorable progress of time in these final scenes is not just felt through our access to the family's anguish, but through our knowledge that Wolfgang, unattended and quite possibly injured in the scuffle with Michael, is still locked in the basement. The key question as to his wellbeing, indeed whether or not he is even still alive, is never answered. Interestingly, the film's ending seems to acknowledge a kind of structural inversion of our typical experience of such stories in our day-to-day lives; the discovery of horror is usually the catalyst for the media excavation of its extent. However, Schleinzer's film concludes at the moment of revelation. Amid sorting through Michael's belongings, his mother walks downstairs in search of more boxes and bags. Later in the day she ventures down again, this time noticing the locked blue door. Teasingly, the film ends, cutting to black when she has opened it just wide enough to peer inside, a deliberate frustration to the viewer's want of closure.

By not only giving us the shock of sudden violent disruption, but by contemplating the everyday's absorption of it in the persistence of a world indifferent, the films in this chapter call attention to the nature of everyday time and the narrative parameters we impose in order to make it mean. In differing ways, both *I Stand Alone* and *Michael* highlight our need to impose a concordant narrative structure to human experience, to vest it with meaning and render it tolerable. Their ability to disturb, however, comes in the undermining of these narratives, elucidating the naïveté of our credulity in them. Further, the culminating violence that seems to imperil the ordinary, the peripeteia that defies expectations, that we feel should enlighten us to something real (Kermode 2000: 18), is instead absorbed into 'the eternal, pitiless recurrence of things' (Braudel 1980: 11).

The duality of everyday time evoked in *I Stand Alone* and *Michael* – both eventful and linear, but simultaneously non-cumulative and enduring – encapsulates the everyday's fundamental indeterminacy. Everyday time is a paradox, as Blanchot recognises, nothing happens, but something is always happening (1993: 241). By presenting and then undermining the narratives we impose to make the everyday meaningful, *I Stand Alone* and *Michael* throw the extreme and the everyday into tension in varying ways. In Noé's film, the narrativisation of time is an oppressive weight, inflicted on the viewer via the butcher's vitriolic and self-fulfilling declarations of the world's harsh indifference, culminating in his seizing control via decisive, violent action. Where the overturning of this logic as realised in the film's closing moments ostensibly offers a welcome release – palpable in the film's radical shift in aesthetic – the film's disturbing quality comes in the troubling implication that to surrender one's belief in a concordant structure is to accept the everyday as indeterminate and not beholden to one's imposed expectations of it. Schleinzer's film, by contrast, assumes the ambiguity of the everyday from its opening moments, presenting us with a world in which the violent and the banal are already and always entangled. Deepening our understanding of this dynamic through a motif gesture that in varied ways filters violence through the everyday, the film incites our want for these to be isolated opposites, while continually eroding our attempts to render them such.

By showing the endurance of the everyday in the wake of disruptive violence, what a return to the everyday might look like, and indeed throwing into doubt the very notion that the everyday and violence are at all separate, these films make explicit what is implicit in the films discussed in previous chapters – that is, the fallacy of the stories we tell to make sense of our time *in media res*. These films point to something beyond themselves, showing us what is ventured in giving up that narrative safety of eventful, concordant time and accepting the experience of a world that is not beholden to cosmic laws of right and wrong that might be answered – ultimately a world that appears as 'puzzling, indeterminate, ambiguous, and without a guiding structure' (Wilson 1988: 90). In presenting us with a vision of a world that persists unabated, part of the purchase these films have on our imagination and experience is in their giving cause to reflect on the susceptibility of our own everyday outside of the cinema, and to question precisely what is at stake in our narrativisation of time as a means of insulation from indeterminacy.

NOTES

1. Notably, the butcher's name, Phillipe Chavalier, is referred to only once: in a brief shot of his identification documents in the montage that introduces him. Aside from this, he remains essentially nameless, consistent with his self-identification as a kind of everyman figure.
2. As critics have pointed out, Noé's warning countdown at the film's climax is inspired by William Castle's inclusion of a 'fright break' in *Homicidal* (1961). See Hoberman (1999: 125); Romney (1999: A8); Smith (1998: 154).

CONCLUSION

Looking Back

Irreversible (Noé 2002)

> The light which puts out our eyes is darkness to us. Only that day dawns to which we are awake. There is more day to dawn. The sun is but a morning star. (Henry David Thoreau, *Walden*, 243)

> ... the world must be regained every day, in repetition, regained as gone. (Stanley Cavell, *In Quest of the Ordinary*, 172)

An off-duty soldier walking down a busy London street one afternoon is hit by a car whose occupants immediately get out to hack him to death with a meat cleaver. An international student studying in Montreal and working part-time at a convenience store is reported missing before a video of his murder, dismemberment and post-mortem sexual degradation surfaces on an online gore site. The eldest son of a Cairns woman visits the family home to be told 'I've killed them', before discovering the bodies of eight of his siblings. The co-pilot of a commercial aircraft bound for Düsseldorf deliberately locks himself in the cockpit to initiate a descent into the French Alps, killing himself and all 149 other passengers and crew aboard.

The stories above, *faits divers* plucked from recent news,[1] exemplify real-life collisions between violence and the everyday. It is a paradox of the everyday that out of the familiar routines and repetitions of daily life erupts the irrational and unpredictable. Nothing happens, but something is always happening. The eventful rears its head, sometimes with devastating consequences, and yet the everyday persists and progresses indifferent.

The films considered in this book capture and aestheticise this paradox – the everyday's 'fruitful ambivalence' – by pitching the familiar and repetitious in tension with the violent and eventful. I claim that this strain gives rise to uncertainty, manifest in a foreclosing of textual containment that precludes us from tethering acts of violence to secure and stable meaning. This may be in the brief intrusions of an uncanny everyday upon worlds in which violence has become omnipresent. At other times, this tension is evident in the refusal to bear access to the subjectivity that might render severe actions legible, or in the stylistic flattening that suggests that murder and suicide are on a par with buying groceries or getting ready for work. Or we may see it play out in the structuring of a film, in the varying degrees of proximity that measure the extent to which these worlds are vulnerable to violent disruption. Alternatively, this tension can find its form in a film's treatment of time, in the contrast between a world that is eventful, linear and comprehensible, and one that is open and indifferent, casting doubt upon the narratives we impose upon it.

The preceding chapters have highlighted this dynamic between violence and the everyday as an experience that hinders aesthetic closure. Violence in these films is often sudden, paroxysmal and world shattering; or, more accurately, it feels like it should be, but isn't. But these films are about ways of experiencing the everyday as aestheticised, as much as they are about ways of experiencing violence as such; as something like a memory that can be accessed and enacted to greater or lesser success in the face of extreme rupture (*Salò* and *Come and See*); as a space where coherence is tauntingly present but kept hidden (*Money* and *The Seventh Continent*); as something that is not self-evident but that must be cultivated and recognised through effort (*Fat Girl*); as foreclosed, without the possibility of openness (*Twentynine Palms* and *Dog Days*); as a shaping and reliable framework in tension with an open and unanchored world becoming (*I Stand Alone* and *Michael*).

What are we to make of the contemporary desire to evoke an everyday that is vulnerable to the threat of irrational and violent disruption? And what is at stake in these images that strip away the sense-making knowledge that we rely on to get through day-to-day life? One way to consider these questions is to reflect upon, as I think these filmmakers would have us do, the everyday we inhabit outside of the cinema. Notably, *Fat Girl* and *The Seventh Continent* were both inspired by news stories, while *Michael* is irrevocably linked to the case of Josef Fritzl.[2] Traditional and social media cultivate an image of the everyday fraught with a pervasive feeling of imminent rupture. We have new levels of accessibility to violent content that is unmediated by news networks; citizen news websites like LiveLeak (formerly the shock site Ogrish) and shock sites like Best Gore and Rotten make access to real graphic imagery simple. Terrorist organisations are also notoriously savvy with social media, distributing professionally produced execution videos and recruitment materials online.

Comparable to the way violence in the films examined shatters our sense of complacency, Terry Eagleton considers the terrorist impulse to be as much an attack on meaning as it is on material existence. According to Eagleton, in a world that is growing increasingly 'depthless, transparent, rationalized and instantly communicable', the ruthless murder of innocent civilians 'reinstates the opaque, the excessive, the irreducibly particular' (2005: 91). Terrorism, particularly suicide bombing, employs violence as an attack on rationality; by distorting the everyday beyond recognition, the terrorist act is 'the ultimate act of defamiliarization' (ibid.: 92).

Curiously, grand narratives of the world's origin and interpretation are also being invoked as the means through which radical violence breaks into the everyday. Josie Appleton argues that in a vacuum of meaning (a product of secular Western modernity), grand narratives are being recruited by lone citizens as something to give shape to extreme responses to situations that are, in actuality, banal. At least this seems an accurate assessment in the case of the delivery driver who used ISIS as a reason to behead his boss days after being reprimanded for dropping equipment from a palette.[3] As Appleton states: 'Workplace disputes are transmuted into the terms of some grand religious clash, whereas they in fact remain in all their banality as a workplace dispute. The abstraction of an "IS attack" is stuck like an afterthought on violence of the basest particularity' (Appleton 2016).

In both Eagleton's example of the suicide bomber, and Appleton's interpretation of the tendency for individuals to retroactively extrapolate disproportionate responses to banal disagreements, the relationship between violence and meaning is fraught. In Eagleton's reading, violence is employed as an irrational opposition to the patterns and expectations of everyday life. What is experienced as ordered and familiar is susceptible to its opposite: the chaotic and unexpected. In Appleton's assessment, several recent instances of violence that have been attributed to religious devotion are in fact examples of individuals scrabbling for ideologies in the wake of a contemporary void of traditional beliefs. In this sense, arch narratives that explain a world in conflict are desperately sought to make violence mean.

To attribute or even compare the prevalence of this tendency in contemporary European art cinema to a Western experience of the everyday outside of it, is necessarily speculative. It is to try to look back at something that is still in progress. Perhaps we are seeing these films find their currency in a contemporary feeling of deep uncertainty. Perhaps it is something else entirely. It is at least possible that what they are discovering in the onscreen connection of violence and the everyday is the threat of scepticism as a renewable, modern resource. As this book draws to a close, I want to consider a final iteration of this tension between the lightning and the banal that reveals the everyday in its fruitful ambivalence. *Irreversible*, Gaspar Noé's backward-running revenge-rape narrative, structurally absorbs the desire to look backwards – not at traumatic spectacle as in *Come and See* and *Salò*, but at the everyday through the lens of violent rupture. In contrast to the films examined in the earlier chapters, it is the trajectory away from violence towards the everyday in *Irreversible* that renders the violence legible. And yet, the everyday we arrive at, at the film's close, is imbued with the violence that has gone before.

MOURNING THE WORLD: THE EVERYDAY AS TRANSCENDENT, THE EVERYDAY AS LOST IN *IRREVERSIBLE*

> Once there were brook trout in the streams in the mountains. You could see them standing in the amber current where the white edges of their fins wimpled softly in the flow. They smelled of moss in your hand. Polished and muscular and torsional. On their backs were vermiculate patterns that were maps of the world in its becoming. Maps and mazes. Of a thing which could not be put back. Not be made right again. In the deep glens where they lived all things were older than man and they hummed of mystery. (Cormac McCarthy, *The Road*, 306–7)

The final paragraph of Cormac McCarthy's *The Road* describes details of a world that is already lost. At the beginning of the novel, the world as we know it has already disappeared, quite literally, to some unnamed catastrophic event that leaves its protagonists to traverse a treacherous post-apocalyptic landscape in a bid to survive. In spite of the bleakness of a world erased, McCarthy's language here reaches back to mourn an everyday that is steeped in profundity. Somewhere in the sensory perception of these trout, their look in the current, their smell and feel in the hand, is access to something deeper and more essential than human understanding. In attending to the particulars we might but glimpse it – what Emerson referred to as the 'one design [that] unites the farthest pinnacle and the lowest trench' (1982: 102). Or, more accurately in McCarthy's prose, we might have glimpsed it if we had taken the care to look sooner.

On one hand, McCarthy's evocation of a biblical prose and all-consuming struggles between good and evil is, as Amy Hungerford (2008) has argued, a means of extending the longevity of the text's impact. Implicit, however, is that in order to get at the essence of human existence, to discover and separate what truly matters, McCarthy also erases the world. What remains is this transcendent imagery of trout in a stream; for McCarthy here, the key to transcendence is in the ordinary world that we dismiss day-to-day.

I want to consider this experience of the world as lost in another text that operates in grandiose terms, and whose grandiosity similarly functions in its extension of the film world beyond the immediacy of our encounter with it. Like McCarthy's prose in *The Road*, Gaspar Noé's *Irreversible* plays out its characters' struggles with what seems to be an apocalyptic finality, and yet part of its quality as a text that stays with us can be attributed to its decision to look backwards at the everyday that is lost at the outset.

Irreversible begins with an ending. The reverse chronological structure means that we enter the film's world disorientated. The camera whirls unanchored and events are presented with little context. Sirens blare on a Paris street at night. An unconscious man is wheeled out of a club on a stretcher. Later in the film, that is, earlier in the narrative, we see this same man, Marcus, attempt to navigate a labyrinthine gay sex club, enraged and searching for someone for reasons as yet unclear. His friend Pierre follows in a futile attempt to defuse Marcus' escalating anger. The scene is hellish; the camera twists in uneven and dizzying motion, catching glimpses here and there of the characters under red light and heavy shadow. The soundscape is similarly chaotic, a repetitive series of crescendos and decrescendos, unrelenting waves of mechanical noise. Thinking he has located the man he is looking for, Marcus smashes a bottle across a stranger's face and a fight erupts. Pushed to the ground, Marcus' arm is bent back behind his body and snapped. When the stranger begins unbuckling his belt, fixing to rape Marcus, a formerly passive Pierre steps in, pulverising the culprit's face with a fire extinguisher in graphic detail, the camera charting the momentum of each blow.

To return to Lesley Stern's axis of the everyday, style and content are both histrionic here, running at fever pitch. Brutality irrupts without context, the world already contaminated by violent impulses that we are not given the framework to comprehend. Our understanding of the events only gradually becomes clear as we retreat back through the narrative timeline: the altercation in the club is a response to the protracted brutal rape and beating of Marcus' girlfriend, Alex. The film itself operates on a kind of continuum – at one end a chaotic frenzy of violence bereft of a framework to render it legible, at the other, a serene and transcendent vision of the everyday that is inflected with the violence that has preceded it. In this way, we are not left with violence without clarity as in *Hidden* and *Fat Girl*, rather it is the film's trajectory away from violence and towards the everyday that gives its violence meaning. However, this has the implicit effect of colouring our experience of the everyday with the knowledge of what has come before.

Irreversible ends with a beginning. Marcus and Alex awaken in their apartment from an afternoon nap to the telephone's incessant ringing. The colour palette is warm, the mood lackadaisical. Slowly emerging from the depths of sleep, the naked couple stretch and play, alternately cuddling, teasing and wrestling. By lamplight, Marcus puts on a record and the pair dance, embrace and laugh, finally gathering themselves to ready for the night out that we already know will end in tragedy. There is an intimacy born of genuine familiarity here; the two performers (Vincent Cassel and Monica Bellucci) were married at the time of production, their relaxed play unfolding in long take over a ten-minute period before Marcus steps out to buy drinks for the evening. In a private moment, Alex conducts a pregnancy test and we watch her response change from a nervous chuckle to quiet contemplation as she processes this information that will presumably shape the rest of her life.

It's here that Noé's stylistic treatment of the everyday begins to shift from a relaxed observation of micro events to the more grandiose and inflated formalism familiar from the film's opening. The solemn and imposing notes of Beethoven's Symphony No. 7 in A Opus 92 rise on the soundtrack and the camera slowly turns up to the ceiling, signalling another transition back to an earlier point in the narrative timeline. Briefly, the camera declines to show Alex asleep, her hand on her belly as though already subconsciously aware of her pregnancy, before veering off again in a vertiginous motion out of the room's window. For a few seconds the camera is swept aloft, tracing clouds in the sky before winding downwards again and settling momentarily on an inverted view of Alex reposed and reading in a park (see Figure 6.1).

It's an everyday image, but one that is stylistically inflated. From this brief moment of stillness, the camera ascends again, arching upwards to give a bird's-eye view. Surrounded by other sunbathers, Alex's setting appears too perfectly choreographed to have just happened – the grass is resplendent, small children run through a sprinkler in ecstatic play trailing kites behind them, followed quickly by an excited puppy.

In discussing McCarthy's transcendent image of the trout, I described the way in which image accrues a gravitas via both its retrospective position in the narrative – its prelapsarian look back at a world already lost – and its overt stylisation through ornate prose. Noé's *Irreversible* functions in a similar way. Where a film like Breillat's *Fat Girl* carries this threat of loss within its

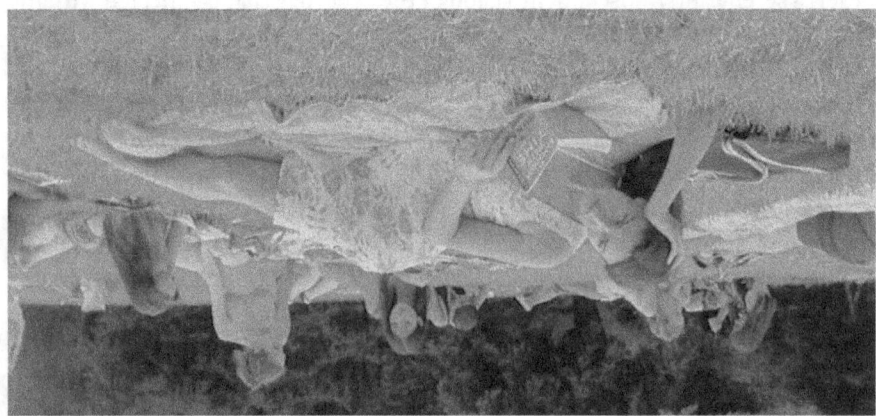

Figure 6.1: The everyday upturned in *Irreversible*.

everydayness, *Irreversible* seems reliant upon our experience of the extreme potential of our world to rupture, in order to afford the everyday its proper weight. In *Irreversible*, the everyday has already been devastated, and yet, like the final passage in *The Road*, we are not given the vocabulary with which to gain a precise sense of what has been lost until it's too late. We experience the everyday in its transcendent beauty, but this is held at odds with the knowledge that this is 'a thing which [can] not be put back. Not be made right again.'

However, as Hungerford points out, there is a contradiction in McCarthy's assertion about the irretrievability of the world, because his words carry hope. It is McCarthy's words 'that put the speckled trout back into the river and the river back into the valley and make things right again even as the words say these things cannot be done' (Hungerford 2010: 135–6). I want to suggest that Noé's evocation of the everyday at the close of *Irreversible* is likewise fraught with competing impulses; the dual nature of the everyday as present, and our experience of it as already lost embodies what Cavell (1982: 177) observes as the equation between 'morning (as dawning) and mourning (as grieving)' at the close of Thoreau's *Walden*: 'The sun is but a morning star.' For Cavell, Thoreau's parting image both suggests of our potential, and entails our experience of loss.

While we might be inclined to take Noé's ending as ultimately pessimistic – the everyday is held up as an object for mourning – I think this would be an incomplete reading of the film. *Irreversible*'s motto – Time destroys all things (repeated at the film's end) – seems to foreclose the everyday as without the possibility for renewal, and yet Noé also showcases the everyday as a vital and beautiful realm of potential. Unlike the world of *Twentynine Palms* described in Chapter 4, which seems sealed off from the positive potential of the everyday, *Irreversible*, for all its ruthlessness, articulates the everyday as something *worth* putting back together again. It is in erasing the film world that Noé is able to give voice to, and have us reflect upon, what truly matters in our own.

Troubled Everyday has been an attempt to expand the way we might think about violence in contemporary European art cinema and, in doing so, to reconsider the boundaries between the ordinary and the extreme. What unites the films under discussion is the conversation that is struck between the everyday and the eventful, the banal and those brief but acutely registered disruptions that tear a fissure in our understanding and gesture towards something beyond themselves. That these moments manage to throw us not only into some immediate visceral response but one that permeates our experience after the films have ended is telling of just what is at stake in the expectations we hold and the stories we tell. Such moments seem bound to convey something educative – to elucidate the narrative, better yet the world we take such narratives to reflect. That these moments consistently refuse to reveal their purpose, to be the 'lightning that illuminates the banal', is intensely seductive. But it is also deeply troubling.

NOTES

1. Referring respectively to the following cases: the murder of Lee Rigby in London in May 2013 by Michael Adebolajo and Michael Adebowale; the murder and decapitation of Lin Jun in May 2012 in Montreal by Luka Magnotta; the murders of eight children in December 2014 in Cairns by Raina Mersane Ina Thaiday; and the deliberate crashing of Germanwings Flight 9525 in the French Alps in March 2015 by Andreas Lubitz.
2. Josef Fritzl made news headlines in April 2008 when it came to light that he had imprisoned his daughter Elisabeth at age eighteen in a concealed room in the family home's basement in Amstetten, Austria for twenty-four years. During this period of captivity he repeatedly raped her, resulting in the births of seven children.
3. Referring to the case of Yassine Salhi who decapitated his boss, Hervé Cornara in St-Quentin-Fallavier in June 2015.

Works Cited

Adamowicz, Elza (2010), *Un Chien Andalou: French Film Guide*, London: I. B. Tauris.
Aitken, Ian (2006), *Realist Film Theory and Cinema: The Nineteenth-Century Lukácsian and Intuitionist Realist Traditions*, Manchester: Manchester University Press.
Aldama, Frederick Luis and Herbert Lindenberger (2016), *Aesthetics of Discomfort: Conversations on Disquieting Art*, Michigan: University of Michigan Press.
Altman, Rick (ed.) (1992), *Sound Theory Sound Practice*, New York: Routledge.
Appleton, Josie (2016), 'Terrorism and the Crisis of Western Culture', https://notesonfreedom.com/2016/01/15/terrorism-and-the-crisis-of-western-culture/, accessed 7 May 2016.
Barr, Charles (1972), '*Straw Dogs, A Clockwork Orange* and the Critics', *Screen* 13:2, 17–31.
Bataille, Georges (1986 [1957]), *Erotism: Death and Sensuality*, trans. Mary Dalwood, San Francisco: City Lights.
Baudry, Jean-Louis (1986), 'Ideological Effects of the Basic Apparatus', in Philip Rosen (ed.), *Narrative, Apparatus, Ideology: A Film Theory Reader*, New York: Columbia University Press, pp. 286–98.
Béar, Liza (2008), *Beyond the Frame: Dialogues With World Filmmakers*, Westport: Praeger.
Berlant, Lauren (2011), *Cruel Optimism*, Durham, NC: Duke University Press.
Beugnet, Martine (2007), *Cinema and Sensation: French Film and the Art of Transgression*, Edinburgh: Edinburgh University Press.
Blanchot, Maurice (1993 [1969]), *The Infinite Conversation*, trans. Susan Hanson, Minneapolis: University of Minnesota Press.
Bondanella, Peter (2009), *A History of Italian Cinema*, New York: Continuum.
Booth, Michael (2004), '"Twentynine Palms" shocks without value', *Denver Post*, 11 June, p. F.05.
Bordwell, David (1986), *Narration in the Fiction Film*, London: Routledge.
— (1989), *Making Meaning: Inference and Rhetoric in the Interpretation of Cinema*, Cambridge, MA: Harvard University Press.
Boyum, Joy Gould (1977), 'How Far Can Art Go?', *Wall Street Journal*, 10 October, p. 15.
Bradshaw, Peter (2001), 'The First Seduction', *The Guardian*, 7 December, https://www.theguardian.com/culture/2001/dec/07/artsfeatures2, accessed 23 June 2016.
Bradshaw, Peter (2003), 'Time of the Wolf', *The Guardian*, 17 October, https://www.theguardian.com/film/2003/oct/17/michael-haneke-isabelle-huppert, accessed 23 June 2016.

Braudel, Fernand (1980), *On History*, trans. Sarah Matthews, London: Weidenfeld & Nicolson.
Bresson, Robert (1996), *Notes on the Cinematographer*, trans. Jonathan Griffin, London: Quartet.
Brinkema, Eugenie (2014), *The Forms of the Affects*, Durham, NC: Duke University Press.
Brunette, Peter (2010), *Michael Haneke*, Urbana: University of Illinois Press.
Burr, Ty (2004), 'Explicit "Palms" is More Silly Than Shocking', *Boston Globe*, 16 July, http://archive.boston.com/news/globe/living/articles/2004/07/16/explicit_palms_is_more_silly_than_shocking/?comments=all, accessed 23 June 2016.
Canby, Vincent (1976), 'Explicit Violence Overwhelms Every Other Value On the Screen', *The New York Times*, 17 October, p. 69+.
Canby, Vincent (1977a), '"Salo" is Disturbing ...', *The New York Times*, 1 October, p. 11.
Canby, Vincent (1977b), 'Seen Any "Accessible" Movies Lately?', *New York Times*, 9 October, p. D15+.
Carroll, Noël (2008), *The Philosophy of Motion Pictures*, Malden: Blackwell Publishing.
Carroll, Robert and Stephen Prickett (eds) (2008), *The Bible: Authorized King James Version with Apocrypha*, Oxford: Oxford University Press.
Cavell, Stanley (1982), 'Politics as Opposed to What?', *Critical Inquiry* 9:1, 157–78.
— (1988), *In Quest of the Ordinary: Lines of Skepticism and Romanticism*, Chicago: University of Chicago Press.
— (1999), *The Claim of Reason: Wittgenstein, Skepticism, Morality, and Tragedy*, Oxford: Oxford University Press.
Chion, Michel (2002), *Eyes Wide Shut*, trans. Trista Selous, London: British Film Institute.
Chrisafis, Angelique (2002), 'Why Should We Be Regularly Exposed to Graphic Scenes of Murder, but be Spared Rape?', *The Guardian*, 23 October, p. A8.
Church, David (2009), 'Of Manias, Shit, and Blood: The Reception of *Salò* as a "Sick Film"', *Participations: Journal of Audience & Reception Studies* 6:2, 340–72.
Clayton, Alex (2011), 'Coming to Terms', in Alex Clayton and Andrew Klevan (eds), *The Language and Style of Film Criticism*, Abingdon: Routledge, pp. 27–37.
Coplan, Amy (2009), 'Empathy and Character Engagement', in Livingston, Paisley and Carl Plantinga (eds), *The Routledge Companion to Philosophy and Film*, Abingdon: Routledge, pp. 97–110.
Coulthard, Lisa (2009), 'Ethical Violence: Suicide as Authentic Act in the films of Michael Haneke', in Ben McCann and David Sorfa (eds), *The Cinema of Michael Haneke: Europe Utopia*, London: Wallflower, pp. 38–48.
— (2010a), 'Desublimating Desire: Courtly Love and Catherine Breillat', *Journal for Cultural Research* 14:1, 57–69.
— (2010b), 'Uncanny Horrors: Male Rape in Bruno Dumont's *Twentynine Palms*', in Dominique Russell (ed.), *Rape in Art Cinema*, New York: Continuum, pp. 171–84.
— (2011), 'Interrogating the Obscene: Extremism and Michael Haneke', in Tanya Horeck and Tina Kendall (eds), *The New Extremism in Cinema: From France to Europe*, Edinburgh: Edinburgh University Press, pp. 180–91.
de Certeau, Michel (1984 [1980]), *The Practice of Everyday Life*, trans. Steven Rendall, Berkeley: University of California Press.
Denby, David (2004), 'Feel the Earth', *The New Yorker*, 12 April, http://www.newyorker.com/magazine/2004/04/12/feel-the-earth, accessed 23 June 2016.
Dumont, Bruno (2004), 'Work Notes', trans. Joann Mitchell, http://www.landmarktheaters.com/mn/twentynine_palms.html, accessed 8 July 2012.
Eagleton, Terry (2005), *Holy Terror*, Oxford: Oxford University Press.

Ebert, Roger (2009a), 'Cannes #5: Even Now Already is it in the World', 17 May, http://www.rogerebert.com/rogers-journal/cannes-5-even-now-already-is-it-in-the-world, accessed 4 May 2016.
— (2009b), 'Cannes #6: A Devil's Advocate for "Antichrist"', 19 May, http://www.rogerebert.com/rogers-journal/cannes-6-a-devils-advocate-for-antichrist, accessed 4 May 2016.
Elsaesser, Thomas (2005), *European Cinema: Face to Face with Hollywood*, Amsterdam: Amsterdam University Press.
Emerson, Ralph Waldo (1982 [1837]), 'The American Scholar', in Larzer Ziff (ed.), *Selected Essays*, New York: Penguin.
Falcon, Richard (1999), 'Reality is Too Shocking', *Sight and Sound* 9:1, 10–13.
Felski, Rita (2013), 'Introduction', *New Literary History* 33:4, 607–22.
Ferguson, Frances (2004), *Pornography, the Theory: What Utilitarianism Did to Action*, Chicago: University of Chicago Press.
Fowler, Catherine (ed.) (2002), *The European Cinema Reader*, London: Routledge.
Fox-Kales, Emily (2010), '*À ma soeur!*: Erotic Bodies and the Primal Scene Reconfigured', *Journal for Cultural Research* 14:1, 15–26.
Gallafent, Ed (2005), 'The Dandy and the Magdalen: Interpreting the Long Take in Hitchcock's *Under Capricorn* (1949)', in John Gibbs and Douglas Pye (eds), *Style and Meaning: Studies in the Detailed Analysis of Film*, Manchester: Manchester University Press, pp. 68–84.
Gentileschi, Orazio (1622), *Lot and His Daughters*. Oil on canvas. The J. Paul Getty Museum, Los Angeles.
Gibbs, John and Douglas Pye (eds) (2005), *Style and Meaning: Studies in the Detailed Analysis of Film*, Manchester: Manchester University Press.
Goddard, Michael (2011), 'Eastern Extreme: The Presentation of Eastern Europe as a Site of Monstrosity in *La Vie nouvelle* and *Import/Export*', in Tanya Horeck and Tina Kendall (eds), *The New Extremism in Cinema: From France to Europe*, Edinburgh: Edinburgh University Press, pp. 82–92.
Gregg, Melissa and Gregory J. Seigworth (eds) (2010), *The Affect Theory Reader*, Durham, NC: Duke University Press.
Groen, Rick (2001), 'Seething Sibling Revelry', *Globe and Mail*, 21 February, http://www.theglobeandmail.com/arts/seething-sibling-revelry/article1333860/, accessed 23 June 2016.
Grønstad, Asbjørn (2007), 'Abject Desire: *Anatomie de l'enfer* and the Unwatchable', *Studies in European Cinema* 6:3, 161–9.
— (2011), 'On The Unwatchable', in Tanya Horeck and Tina Kendall (eds), *The New Extremism in Cinema: From France to Europe*, Edinburgh: Edinburgh University Press, pp. 192–205.
— (2012), *Screening the Unwatchable: Spaces of Negation in Post-Millennial Art Cinema*, Basingstoke: Palgrave Macmillan.
Harries, Martin (2007), *Forgetting Lot's Wife: On Destructive Spectatorship*, New York: Fordham University Press.
Heiser, Jörg (2003), 'Pulp Fiction: Thomas Demand', *Frieze Magazine*, 3 March, http://friezenewyork.com/article/pulp-fiction?language=de, accessed 23 June 2016.
Hoberman, James (1999), 'Meat and Greet', *The Village Voice*, 23 March, p. 125.
— (2001), 'The Flesh is Bleak', *The Village Voice*, 9 October, http://www.villagevoice.com/film/the-flesh-is-bleak-6396032, accessed 4 May 2016.
Honeycutt, Kirk (2001), 'Strong Sister Act Stumbles', *Hollywood Reporter*, 13 February, n.p.

Horeck, Tanya and Tina Kendall (eds) (2011), *The New Extremism in Cinema: From France to Europe*, Edinburgh: Edinburgh University Press.

Horeck, Tanya (2010), 'Shame and the Sisters: Catherine Breillat's *À ma soeur!* (Fat Girl)', in Dominique Russell (ed.), *Rape in Art Cinema*, New York: Continuum, pp. 195–209.

Hungerford, Amy (2008), 'Lecture 18: Cormac McCarthy, Blood Meridian (cont.)', [PDF document], http://oyc.yale.edu/english/engl-291/lecture-18#transcript, accessed 7 May 2016.

— (2010), *Postmodern Belief: American Literature and Religion Since 1950*, Princeton: Princeton University Press.

Indiana, Gary (2000), *Salò or The 120 Days of Sodom*, London: Palgrave Macmillan.

Jauss, Hans Robert (1982), *Toward an Aesthetic of Reception*, trans. Timothy Bahti, Brighton: Harvester.

Jay, Martin (1984), *Marxism and Totality: The Adventures of a Concept from Lukács to Habermas*, Cambridge: Polity.

Jones, Kent (1999), *L'Argent*, London: British Film Institute.

Kater, Michael H. (2000), *Composers of the Nazi Era: Eight Portraits*, Oxford: Oxford University Press.

Kermode, Frank (2000), *The Sense of an Ending: Studies in the Theory of Fiction*, Oxford: Oxford University Press.

Klemesrud, Judy (1977), 'Film Festival's Fare is Rated Best in Years, and So Are the Parties', *The New York Times*, 4 October, p. 43.

Klevan, Andrew (2000), *Disclosure of the Everyday: Undramatic Achievement in Narrative Film*, Trowbridge: Flicks.

Kuttenberg, Eva (2011), 'Allegory in Michael Haneke's *The Seventh Continent*', in Robert von Dassanowsky and Oliver C. Speck (eds), *New Austrian Film*, New York: Berghahn, pp. 151–65.

Lawton, Anna (1992), *Kinoglasnost: Soviet Cinema in Our Time*, Cambridge: Cambridge University Press.

Lefebvre, Henri (2008 [1947–81]), *Critique of Everyday Life*. 3 vols., trans. John Moore and Gregory Elliott, New York: Verso.

Leiris, Michel (1988 [1938]), 'The Sacred in Everyday Life', trans. Betsy Wing, in Dennis Hollier (ed.), *The College of Sociology (1937–39)*, Minneapolis: University of Minnesota Press, pp. 24–31.

Livingston, Paisley and Carl Plantinga (eds) (2009), *The Routledge Companion to Philosophy and Film*, Abingdon: Routledge.

Lovell, Terry (1983), *Pictures of Reality: Aesthetics, Politics and Pleasure*, London: British Film Institute.

Lübecker, Nikolaj (2007), 'The Dedramatization of Violence in Claire Denis's *I Can't Sleep*', *Paragraph* 30:2, 17–33.

— (2011a), 'Bruno Dumont's *Twentynine Palms*: The Avant-Garde as Tragedy?', *Studies in French Cinema* 11:3, 235–47.

— (2011b), 'Lars von Trier's *Dogville*: A Feel-Bad Film', in Tanya Horeck and Tina Kendall (eds), *The New Extremism in Cinema: From France to Europe*, Edinburgh: Edinburgh University Press, pp. 157–68.

— (2015), *The Feel-Bad Film*, Edinburgh: Edinburgh University Press.

Lukács, Georg (1971 [1920]), *The Theory of the Novel: A Historico-Philosophical Essay on the Forms of Great Epic Literature*, trans. Anna Bostock, London: Merlin.

— (1974 [1910]), *Soul and Form*, trans. Anna Bostock, Cambridge, MA: MIT Press.

Maddock, Trevor H. and Ivan Krisjansen (2002), 'Surrealist Poetics and the Cinema of Evil:

'The Significance of the Expression of Sovereignty in Catherine Breillat's *A Ma Soeur*', *Studies in French Cinema* 3:3, pp. 161-71.
Maggi, Armando (2009), *The Resurrection of the Body: Pier Paolo Pasolini from Saint Paul to Sade*, Chicago: University of Chicago Press.
Malcolm, Derek (1977), 'Pasolini's Awful Masterpiece', *The Guardian*, 14 July, p. 10.
Margulies, Ivone (1996), *Nothing Happens: Chantal Akerman's Hyperrealist Everyday*, Durham, NC: Duke University Press.
Matheou, Demetrios (2005), 'Fear at Ennui's End', *Sight and Sound* 15:8, 17–18.
McCarthy, Cormac (2009 [2006]), *The Road*, London: Picador.
Metz, Christian (1982), *The Imaginary Signifier: Psychoanalysis and the Cinema*, trans. Celia Britton, Annwyl Williams, Ben Brewster and Alfred Guzzetti, Bloomington: Indiana University Press.
Meyer, Carla (2001), 'A Sisterhood Both Powerful and Bitter: "Fat Girl" an Extraordinary Inquiry into Sex', *SFGate*, http://www.sfgate.com/movies/article/A-sisterhood-both-powerful-and-bitter-Fat-2848013.php, accessed 4 May 2016.
Michaels, Lloyd (2008), '*Come and See* (1985): Klimov's Intimate Epic', *Quarterly Review of Film and Video* 25:3, 212–18.
Moore, Rachel O. (2000), *Savage Theory: Cinema as Modern Magic*, Durham, NC: Duke University Press.
Mulvey, Laura (1989), *Visual and Other Pleasures*, Basingstoke: Palgrave Macmillan.
Nabokov, Vladimir (1980 [1955]), *Lolita*, London: Penguin.
Nair, Kartik (2009), '*Caché* and the Secret Image', *Wide Screen* 1.1, http://widescreenjournal.org/index.php/journal/article/viewFile/65/108, accessed 3 December 2015.
Nancy, Jean Luc (2005), *The Ground of the Image*, trans. Jeff Fort, New York: Fordham University Press.
Nesselson, Lisa (2004), 'Review: *Twentynine Palms*', *Variety* 392:4, 34–5.
O'Hehir, Andrew (2002), '*Trouble Every Day*', *Salon* 7 March, http://www.salon.com/2002/03/06/trouble_2/, accessed 25 February 2016.
Onstad, Katrina (2003), 'A Story That's More Tragic Than Titillating', *National Post* 21 February, p. PM6.
Palmer, Tim (2006), 'Style and Sensation in the Contemporary French Cinema of the Body', *Journal of Film and Video* 58:3, 22–32.
— (2011), *Brutal Intimacy: Analyzing Contemporary French Cinema*, Middletown: Wesleyan University Press.
Perkins, V. F. (1993), *Film as Film: Understanding and Judging Movies*, New York: Da Capo.
Petley, Julian (1984), 'Two or Three Things I Know about Video Nasties', *Monthly Film Bulletin* 51:600, 350–2.
Pipolo, Tony (2010), *Robert Bresson: A Passion for Film*, New York: Oxford University Press.
Plantinga, Carl and Greg M. Smith (eds) (1999), *Passionate Views: Film Cognition and Emotion*, Baltimore: Johns Hopkins University Press.
Plantinga, Carl (2009a), 'Emotion and Affect', in Livingston, Paisley and Carl Plantinga (eds), *The Routledge Companion to Philosophy and Film*, Abingdon: Routledge, pp. 86–96.
— (2009b), 'Spectatorship', in Livingston, Paisley and Carl Plantinga (eds), *The Routledge Companion to Philosophy and Film*, Abingdon: Routledge, pp. 249–59.
Poe, Edgar Allan (2015 [1843]), 'The Black Cat', in *The Complete Tales and Poems of Edgar Allan Poe*, New York: Barnes & Noble, pp. 531–8.
Quandt, James (2004), 'Flesh and Blood: Sex and Violence in Recent French Cinema',

ArtForum International 42:6, https://artforum.com/inprint/issue=200402&id=6199, accessed 23 June 2016.

Rivi, Luisa (2007), *European Cinema After 1989: Cultural Identity and Transnational Production*, New York: Palgrave Macmillan.

Romney, Jonathan (1999), 'Blood Simple', *The Guardian*, 19 March, p. A8.

— (2004), 'Le Sex and Violence', *The Independent*, 12 September, http://www.independent.co.uk/arts-entertainment/films/features/le-sex-and-violence-546083.html, accessed 4 June 2016.

Roud, Richard (1983), 'The Cheerful Pessimist With the Spartan Touch', *The Guardian*, 23 June, p. 11.

Russell, Dennis Eugene (2010), *The Portrayal of Social Catastrophe in the German-Language Films of Austrian Filmmaker Michael Haneke (1942–)*, Lewiston: Mellen.

Sade, Marquis de (1966 [1785]), *The 120 Days of Sodom and Other Writings*, trans. Austryin Wainhouse and Richard Seaver, New York: Grove.

Schrader, Paul (1988), *Transcendental Style in Film: Ozu, Bresson, Dreyer*, New York: Da Capo.

Schwartz, Peter J. (2010), 'The Void at the Center of Things: Figures of Identity in Michael Haneke's Glaciation Trilogy', in Roy Grundmann (ed.), *A Companion to Michael Haneke*, Chichester: Wiley-Blackwell, pp. 337–54.

Sharret, Christopher (2006), 'Michael Haneke and the Discontents of European Culture', *Framework: The Journal of Cinema and Media* 47.2, pp. 6-16.

Shaviro, Steven (1993), *The Cinematic Body*, Minneapolis: University of Minnesota Press.

Sheringham, Michael (2006), *Everyday Life: Theories and Practices from Surrealism to the Present*, Oxford: Oxford University Press.

Silverstone, Roger (1994), *Television and Everyday Life*, London: Routledge.

Smith, Garvin (1998), 'Meat is Murder', *The Village Voice*, 9 June, p. 154.

Smith, Murray (1995), *Engaging Characters: Fiction, Emotion and the Cinema*, Oxford: Oxford University Press.

Sobchack, Vivian (2004), *Carnal Thoughts: Embodiment and Moving Image Culture*, Berkeley: University of California Press.

Sobczynski, Peter (2004), 'Interview with Catherine Breillat', *efilmcritic.com*, http://www.efilmcritic.com/feature.php?feature=1244, accessed 23 June 2016.

Sontag, Susan (1994 [1966]), *Against Interpretation*, London: Vintage.

Speck, Oliver C. (2010), *Funny Frames: The Filmic Concepts of Michael Haneke*, New York: Continuum.

Staiger, Janet (2000), *Perverse Spectators: The Practices of Film Reception*, New York: New York University Press.

Stern, Lesley (2001), 'Paths That Wind Through the Thicket of Things', *Critical Inquiry* 28:1, 317–54.

Stewart, Kathleen (2007), *Ordinary Affects*, Durham, NC: Duke University Press.

Strauss, Bob (2001), 'Insight on Young Love Burns Out: Violent Ending Takes Away From "Fat Girl"', *Los Angeles Daily News*, 23 November, http://articles.philly.com/2001-11-23/entertainment/25320111_1_true-love-fat-girl-endurance, accessed 3 June 2016.

Strick, Philip (1987), 'Idi i Smotri (Come and See)', *Monthly Film Bulletin* March 1, pp. 79–80.

Thomas, Deborah (2000), *Beyond Genre: Melodrama, Comedy and Romance in Hollywood Films*, Moffat: Cameron.

Thoreau, Henry David (1965 [1854]), *Walden and 'Civil Disobedience'*, New York: Airmont.

Toles, George (2001), *A House Made of Light: Essays on the Art of Film*, Detroit: Wayne State University Press.
Tolstoy, Leo (2010 [1911]), 'The Forged Coupon', *The Death of Ivan Ilyich and Other Stories*, trans. Richard Pevear and Larissa Volokhonsky, London: Vintage.
Vogel, Amos (1996), 'Of Nonexisting Continents: The Cinema of Michael Haneke', *Film Comment* 32.4, pp. 73–5.
Wheatley, Catherine (2009), *Michael Haneke's Cinema: The Ethic of the Image*, Oxford: Berghahn.
— (2010), 'Contested Interactions: Watching Catherine Breillat's Scenes of Sexual Violence', *Journal for Cultural Research* 14:1, 27–41.
Williams, Christopher (ed.) (1980), *Realism and the Cinema: A Reader*, London: Routledge.
Williams, Linda Ruth (2001), '*À ma soeur!*', *Sight and Sound* 11:12, 12.
Wilson, George M. (1998), *Narration in Light: Studies in Cinematic Point of View*, Baltimore: Johns Hopkins University Press.
Wojcik, Pamela Robertson (2007), 'Spectatorship and Audience Research', in Cook, Pam (ed.), *The Cinema Book* (3rd edn), London: British Film Institute, pp. 538–44.
Youngblood, Denise J. (2007), *Russian War Films: On the Cinema Front, 1914–2005*, Lawrence: University of Kansas Press.

Filmography

An Andalusian Dog [*Un chien Andalou*] (Luis Buñuel 1929)
Anatomy of Hell [*Anatomie de l'enfer*] (Catherine Breillat 2004)
Antichrist (Lars von Trier 2009)
Atonement (Joe Wright 2007)
Badlands (Terrence Malick 1973)
Bastards [*Les Salauds*] (Claire Denis 2013)
Carne (Gaspar Noé 1991)
Citizen Kane (Orson Welles 1941)
Come and See [*Idi i smotri*] (Elem Klimov 1985)
Diary of a Country Priest [*Journal d'un curé de campagne*] (Robert Bresson 1951)
Dog Days [*Hundstage*] (Ulrich Seidl 2001)
Dogtooth [*Kynodontas*] (Giorgos Lanthimos 2009)
Eyes Wide Shut (Stanley Kubrick 1999)
Fat Girl [*À ma soeur!*] (Catherine Breillat 2001)
Fists in the Pocket [*I pugni in tasca*] (Marco Bellocchio 1965)
From Dusk Till Dawn (Robert Rodriguez 1996)
Frontier(s) [*Frontière(s)*] (Xavier Gens 2007)
Funny Games (Michael Haneke 1997)
Funny Games (Michael Haneke 2007)
Ginger Snaps (John Fawcett 2000)
Hidden [*Caché*] (Michael Haneke 2005)
High Tension [*Haute tension*] (Alexandre Aja 2003)
Hostel (Eli Roth 2005)
Humanity [*L'Humanité*] (Bruno Dumont 1999)
Import/Export (Ulrich Seidl 2007)
In the Realm of the Senses [*Ai no korîda*] (Nagisa Ôshima 1976)
Irreversible [*Irréversible*] (Gaspar Noé 2002)
I Stand Alone [*Seul contre tous*] (Gaspar Noé 1998)
Jeanne Dielman [*Jeanne Dielman, 23 Quai du Commerce, 1080 Bruxelles*] (Chantal Akerman 1975)
Junior Size 36 [*36 fillette*] (Catherine Breillat 1988)
Last Woman, The [*La dernière femme*] (Marco Ferreri 1976)
Late Spring [*Banshun*] (Yasujirô Ozu 1949)

Letter from an Unknown Woman (Max Ophüls 1948)
Life of Jesus [*La vie de Jésus*] (Bruno Dumont 1997)
Loves of a Blonde [*Lásky jedné plavovlásky*] (Miloš Forman 1965)
Marathon Man (John Schlesinger 1976)
Michael (Markus Schleinzer 2011)
Money [*L'argent*] (Robert Bresson 1983)
Mother and the Whore, The [*La maman et la putain*] (Jean Eustache 1973)
My Childhood (Bill Douglas 1972)
My Mother [*Ma Mère*] (Christophe Honoré 2004)
Natural Born Killers (Oliver Stone 1994)
New Life, A [*La vie nouvelle*] (Phillipe Grandrieux 2002)
Paisan [*Paisà*] (Roberto Rossellini 1946)
Perfect Love [*Parfait amour!*] (Catherine Breillat 1996)
Piano Teacher, The [*La Pianiste*] (Michael Haneke 2001)
Possession (Andrzej Zulawski 1981)
Real Young Girl, A [*Une vraie jeune fille*] (Catherine Breillat 1976)
Red Desert [*Il deserto rosso*] (Michelangelo Antonioni 1964)
Romance (Catherine Breillat 1999)
Salò or the 120 Days of Sodom [*Salò o le 120 giornate di Sodoma*] (Pier Paolo Pasolini 1975)
Saw (James Wan 2004)
See the Sea [*Regarde la mer*] (François Ozon 1997)
Seventh Continent, The [*Der siebente Kontinent*] (Michael Haneke 1989)
Shawshank Redemption, The (Frank Darabont 1994)
Straw Dogs (Sam Peckinpah 1971)
Taxi Driver (Martin Scorsese 1976)
Them [*Ils*] (David Moreau and Xavier Palut 2006)
Time of the Wolf [*Le temps du loup*] (Michael Haneke 2003)
To Our Loves [*A nos amours*] (Maurice Pialat 1983)
Tribe, The [*Plemya*] (Myroslav Slaboshpytskyi 2014)
Trouble Every Day (Claire Denis 2001)
Twentynine Palms (Bruno Dumont 2003)
Umberto D (Vittorio De Sica 1952)
Vanishing, The [*Spoorloos*] (George Sluizer 1988)
Weekend (Jean-Luc Godard 1967)
White Ribbon, The [*Das weiße Band*] (Michael Haneke 2009)
Wolf Creek (Greg Mclean 2005)
Yard (Thomas Demand 2001)

Index

aesthetics
    as an approach to analysis, 10, 15n12
    disturbing, 3, 8–11, 18, 20–1, 22, 56–7, 92
    relationship to affect, 8–9, 15n12, 22
    see also style
affect
    and 'new extremism', 9, 14n10, 19–21
    and subjectivity, 8–9
    and temporality, 3, 8, 18, 19–21, 123
    definitions, 8
    relationship to aesthetics, 8–9, 10, 15n12, 22
    theorisation of, 8–9, 14n9
alienation, 6, 53–4, 73, 86, 90, 112
An Andalusian Dog, 20, 21
Anatomy of Hell, 65, 66
Antichrist, 11, 20
Appleton, Josie, 119
Atonement, 44

Badlands, 74
Bastards, 11
Bataille, Georges, 8, 13n7, 14n10
Berlant, Lauren, 91–2
Beugnet, Martine, 4, 9, 14n10, 66, 67, 75
Blanchot, Maurice, 6, 13n7, 115
Braudel, Fernand, 91
Breillat, Catherine, 60–1, 64–5, 66, 80, 84, 85; *see also Fat Girl*
Bresson, Robert, 38, 39, 40, 43, 46, 51, 57n2, 57n3, 58n8, 59n9; *see also Money*; *Diary of a Country Priest*
Brinkema, Eugenie, 8–9

Canby, Vincent, 16–18
Carne, 93
Cavell, Stanley, 6, 7–8, 40, 58n4, 123

Certeau, Michel de, 6, 41, 73
child abuse, 95, 102, 104–6, 107–12, 124n2
cinéma du corps, 4, 21, 63; *see also* 'new extremism'
'cinema of sensation', 4, 14n10, 63, 67; *see also* 'new extremism'
Citizen Kane, 133
Come and See, 18, 23, 30–5, 118
Coulthard, Lisa, 3, 4, 66, 85
'cruel optimism', 91–2, 110; *see also* meaning

Demand, Thomas, 69, 87n5
'destructive spectatorship', 22–3, 28, 32, 33–5
Diary of a Country Priest, 40, 41–2, 53, 58n5, 59n9
'discourse of immediacy', 18, 19–21
disturbing aesthetics, 3, 8–11, 18, 20–1, 22, 55, 56–7, 92
Dog Days, 55, 118
Dogtooth, 10, 57
Dumont, Bruno, 17, 64, 66, 69, 73, 74–5; *see also Twentynine Palms*

Eagleton, Terry, 118–19
Ebert, Roger, 20, 21
Emerson, Ralph Waldo, 6, 7–8, 120
European art cinema
    definitions, 13n2
everyday
    aestheticisation of, 102–5, 121–3
    and profundity, 6, 7–8, 40–1, 54, 90, 103–4, 120
    as film style, 39–43, 46, 52–5
    creative potential of, 6, 78, 79, 80, 82, 94, 103, 123

everyday (cont.)
  definitions, 5–7
  'fruitful ambivalence' of, 5, 7, 46, 55, 117
  'hidden totality' of, 5, 8, 14n8, 40–1, 54, 55, 78, 120
  imposition of narrative structures on, 90–2, 95–100, 106, 110–11, 114, 115–16, 118
  indeterminacy of, 5, 6–7, 46, 54–5, 89, 100, 106, 115–16, 117
  language, 70–4, 75–6, 77–80, 82, 83, 85, 86
  negative conceptions of, 5–6, 55, 73, 90
  objects, 35, 38, 39, 40, 44, 45–6, 47, 50, 51, 78, 109
  positive conceptions of, 6, 40–1, 81, 90, 103, 105
  time, 5, 90–2, 94, 100, 110, 113–15, 118
  see also routine
extremes
  and cinema, 4, 8, 9–10, 13n3, 14n10, 16–21, 22, 35, 60–1, 63, 64–5
  and novelty, 18
  see also 'new extremism'
Eyes Wide Shut, 71, 73, 79

family, 2, 3, 10–11, 38–9, 41, 45, 50, 89–90, 98, 108, 113–15
Fat Girl, 60–3, 64, 65, 66–7, 68, 77–87, 118
'feel-bad film', 4, 9, 13n3, 14n10; see also 'new extremism'
Fists in the Pocket, 10
From Dusk Till Dawn, 66, 67
Frontier(s), 84
Funny Games, 4

genre
  hybridity, 66–7
  orientating structures, 68, 69, 76–7, 81–2, 86, 87n3, 118
  subversion of, 4, 60–1, 66–7, 84
Ginger Snaps, 67
Grønstad, Asbjørn, 4, 9, 21, 67

Haneke, Michael, 19, 39, 44, 45, 46, 107; see also Hidden; Seventh Continent, The
Harries, Martin, 22–3, 29, 32
Hidden, 2–3, 121
'hidden totality' see under everyday
High Tension, 84
Horeck, Tanya, 4, 14n10, 18, 19, 21
Hostel, 67
Humanity, 11, 64, 74
Hungerford, Amy, 120, 123

I Stand Alone, 19, 92–106, 108, 115–16, 118
Import/Export, 21
In the Realm of the Senses, 17
interiority see subjectivity
Irreversible, 19–20, 120–3

Jeanne Dielman, 53–4, 107
Junior Size 36, 65

Kendall, Tina, 4, 14n10, 18, 19, 21
Kermode, Frank, 91, 92
Klevan, Andrew, 39, 40–2, 46, 51, 52–4

language see under everyday
Last Woman, The, 17
Late Spring, 40
Lefebvre, Henri, 6, 90
Leiris, Michel, 77–8, 79, 83
Letter from an Unknown Woman, 44
Life of Jesus, 64
'lightning that illuminates the banal', 5, 7, 90, 123; see also Lukács, Georg
'limit situation', 13n7, 41–2
Lot's wife, 22–3, 28–9, 32, 33–5
Loves of a Blonde, 40
Lübecker, Nikolaj, 4, 9, 13n3, 14n10, 66
Lukács, Georg, 5–6, 8, 14n8

Marathon Man, 17
Margulies, Ivone, 54
McCarthy, Cormac, 120, 122–3
meaning
  and narrative closure, 7, 8, 22, 29, 55–6, 90, 106, 118
  desire for, 2, 56, 91–2, 119
  imposition of, 90–2, 104, 106, 114, 115
  see also scepticism
Michael, 106–16, 118
Money, 37–8, 39, 41, 43–4, 46, 50–2, 54, 56–7, 118
Mother and the Whore, The, 17
murder, 24, 37, 38, 41, 46, 50–1, 53, 60, 62, 63, 64, 65, 76, 84, 87n5, 93, 101, 117, 118, 121, 124n1
music, 36n2, 59n10, 70, 84, 94, 95, 122
  and irony, 29, 47–9, 101
My Childhood, 41
My Mother, 10

Nabokov, Vladimir, 10, 104–5
Natural Born Killers, 74
'new extremism', 4, 9, 17–18, 19–21, 62, 63
'new French extremity', 4, 63; see also 'new extremism'
New Life, A, 21

Noé, Gaspar, 21, 96–9, 101, 106, 116n2, 122, 123; see also Irreversible; I Stand Alone

Paisan, 41
Pasolini, Pier Paolo, 23, 26, 27–8; see also Salò or the 120 Days of Sodom
Perfect Love, 65
performance, 43, 44, 49–50
Piano Teacher, The, 3
Possession, 11

Quandt, James, 4, 17–18, 19, 63
quotidian see everyday

rape see under violence
Real Young Girl, A, 64–5
realism, 7, 40, 53, 54, 58n8
Red Desert, 46
repetition, 38, 41, 53–4, 58n8, 69–73, 77, 86, 107, 112, 117
Romance, 65
routine
　as alienating, 5, 7, 53–5, 112
　disruption of, 5, 13n7, 35, 42, 46–7, 53, 112
　shaping continuity through, 3, 7, 35, 111–12

Sade, Marquis de, 16, 17, 23, 27, 29
Salò or the 120 Days of Sodom, 16–17, 18, 23–30, 32, 90, 118
Saw, 67
scepticism, 6, 40, 92, 119; see also Cavell, Stanley
Schleinzer, Markus, 107; see also Michael
Schrader, Paul, 39–40, 46, 58n8
See the Sea, 63
Seidl, Ulrich, 55; see also Dog Days; Import/Export
Seventh Continent, The, 7, 38–9, 41, 43, 44–50, 53–4, 55–6, 57, 77, 84, 93, 104, 107, 118
Shawshank Redemption, The, 44
Sheringham, Michael, 5, 6–7, 13n7, 90, 103
Smith, Murray, 43
sound, 26–7, 29, 32, 33, 39, 50, 74, 84, 93, 100, 101, 121; see also music
spectatorship
　as internalised, 24–9, 32, 33–5, 56, 80
　theorisation of, 9, 14n11
　see also 'destructive spectatorship'
Stern, Lesley, 42, 53
Straw Dogs, 20
style
　and repetition, 38, 41, 53–4, 58n8, 69–73, 77, 86, 87n5, 107

　as an approach to analysis, 10, 15n12
　as fragmented, 37, 39, 43, 44, 46, 47, 50, 53, 107, 110
　at odds with content, 2, 42–3, 46–51, 57, 58n8, 59n9, 107–8, 118
subjectivity, 43–6, 49–50, 54, 55, 57, 58n4, 73–4, 77, 85, 93, 94, 101, 118; see also performance
suicide, 2–3, 27–9, 39, 45, 47, 49, 56, 93, 101, 102, 104, 117, 118, 119

Taxi Driver, 17
terrorism, 118–19
Them, 84
Thomas, Deborah, 68, 87n3
Thoreau, Henry David, 103, 104, 117, 123
Time of the Wolf, 19
torture, 16, 24, 26–7, 28–9
Tribe, The, 11, 57
Trouble Every Day, 20–1, 63
Twentynine Palms, 4, 17, 55, 61, 62–4, 65, 66–8, 69–77, 82, 84, 85, 86–7, 118, 123

Umberto D, 41, 77
'unwatchable, the', 4, 9, 13n3, 21, 63; see also 'new extremism'

Vanishing, The, 89–90
violence
　and authenticity, 13n7, 92
　as meaningless, 16–18, 60–1, 63–4
　as mechanism to block meaning, 2, 3, 8, 9, 28, 92, 117, 118–19
　as spectacle, 2, 26–7, 29, 31, 33–4, 75–6, 84, 101, 121
　bearing witness to, 26–9, 31–5, 75, 76, 84–5
　filtered through the ordinary, 29–30, 39, 46–7, 51, 59n11, 107–8, 109–14, 118
　sexual, 16, 19, 24, 26, 31, 60, 62, 64, 65, 75, 79, 85, 87n1, 93, 95, 104, 107–8, 121, 124n2
vision
　as motif, 24–9, 32, 45, 58n6
　frustration of, 22–3, 27–9
　see also spectatorship

Weekend, 17, 93
White Ribbon, The, 11
Wilson, George M., 66, 69
Wolf Creek, 74

Yard, 69

EU representative:
Easy Access System Europe
Mustamäe tee 50, 10621 Tallinn, Estonia
Gpsr.requests@easproject.com

www.ingramcontent.com/pod-product-compliance
Lightning Source LLC
Chambersburg PA
CBHW051102230426
43667CB00013B/2414